THE TEACHIN...
William Ayers—*Series Ed...* ...ute *Series Editor*

EDITORIAL BOARD: Hal Adams (1939-20...), Barbara Bowman, Lisa Delpit, Michelle Fine, Maxine Greene (1917–2014), Caroline Heller, Annette Henry, Asa Hilliard (1933–2007), Rashid Khalidi, Kevin K. Kumashiro, Gloria Ladson-Billings, Charles Payne, Luis Rodriguez, Jonathan Silin, William Watkins (1946-2014)

Where Is the Justice? Engaged Pedagogies in Schools and Communities
VALERIE KINLOCH, EMILY A. NEMETH, TAMARA T. BUTLER, & GRACE D. PLAYER

Teacher Educators as Critical Storytellers: Effective Teachers as Windows and Mirrors
ANTONIO L. ELLIS, NICHOLAS D. HARTLEP, GLORIA LADSON-BILLINGS, & DAVID O. STOVALL, EDS.

Surrendered: Why Progressives Are Losing the Biggest Battles in Education
KEVIN K. KUMASHIRO

Holler If You Hear Me, Comic Edition
GREGORY MICHIE & RYAN ALEXANDER-TANNER

Same as It Never Was: Notes on a Teacher's Return to the Classroom
GREGORY MICHIE

Spectacular Things Happen Along the Way: Lessons from an Urban Classroom, Second Edition
BRIAN D. SCHULTZ

Teaching with Conscience in an Imperfect World: An Invitation
WILLIAM AYERS

Worth Striking For: Why Education Policy Is Every Teacher's Concern (Lessons from Chicago)
ISABEL NUÑEZ, GREGORY MICHIE, AND PAMELA KONKOL

Being Bad: My Baby Brother and the School-to-Prison Pipeline
CRYSTAL T. LAURA

Fear and Learning in America: Bad Data, Good Teachers, and the Attack on Public Education
JOHN KUHN

Deep Knowledge: Learning to Teach Science for Understanding and Equity
DOUGLAS B. LARKIN

Bad Teacher! How Blaming Teachers Distorts the Bigger Picture
KEVIN K. KUMASHIRO

Crossing Boundaries—Teaching and Learning with Urban Youth
VALERIE KINLOCH

The Assault on Public Education: Confronting the Politics of Corporate School Reform
WILLIAM H. WATKINS, ED.

Pedagogy of the Poor: Building the Movement to End Poverty
WILLIE BAPTIST & JAN REHMANN

Grow Your Own Teachers: Grassroots Change for Teacher Education
ELIZABETH A. SKINNER, MARIA TERESA GARRETÓN, & BRIAN D. SCHULTZ, EDS.

Girl Time: Literacy, Justice, and the School-to-Prison Pipeline
MAISHA T. WINN

Holler If You Hear Me: The Education of a Teacher and His Students, Second Edition
GREGORY MICHIE

Controversies in the Classroom: A Radical Teacher Reader
JOSEPH ENTIN, ROBERT C. ROSEN, & LEONARD VOGT, EDS.

The Seduction of Common Sense: How the Right Has Framed the Debate on America's Schools
KEVIN K. KUMASHIRO

Teach Freedom: Education for Liberation in the African-American Tradition
CHARLES M. PAYNE & CAROL SILLS STRICKLAND, EDS.

Social Studies for Social Justice: Teaching Strategies for the Elementary Classroom
RAHIMA C. WADE

Pledging Allegiance: The Politics of Patriotism in America's Schools
JOEL WESTHEIMER, ED.

See You When We Get There: Teaching for Change in Urban Schools
GREGORY MICHIE

Echoes of Brown: Youth Documenting and Performing the Legacy of *Brown v. Board of Education*
MICHELLE FINE

Writing in the Asylum: Student Poets in City Schools
JENNIFER MCCORMICK

Teaching the Personal and the Political: Essays on Hope and Justice
WILLIAM AYERS

Teaching Science for Social Justice
ANGELA CALABRESE BARTON ET AL.

THE TEACHING FOR SOCIAL JUSTICE SERIES, *continued*

Putting the Children First:
The Changing Face of Newark's Public Schools
JONATHAN G. SILIN & CAROL LIPPMAN, EDS.

Refusing Racism:
White Allies and the Struggle for Civil Rights
CYNTHIA STOKES BROWN

A School of Our Own: Parents, Power, and
Community at the East Harlem Block Schools
TOM RODERICK

The White Architects of Black Education:
Ideology and Power in America, 1865–1954
WILLIAM WATKINS

The Public Assault on America's Children:
Poverty, Violence, and Juvenile Injustice
VALERIE POLAKOW, ED.

Construction Sites: Excavating Race, Class, and
Gender Among Urban Youths
LOIS WEIS & MICHELLE FINE, EDS.

Walking the Color Line:
The Art and Practice of Anti-Racist Teaching
MARK PERRY

A Simple Justice:
The Challenge of Small Schools
WILLIAM AYERS, MICHAEL KLONSKY, &
GABRIELLE H. LYON, EDS.

Teaching for Social Justice:
A Democracy and Education Reader
WILLIAM AYERS, JEAN ANN HUNT, &
THERESE QUINN

Where Is the Justice?
Engaged Pedagogies in Schools and Communities

Valerie Kinloch
Emily A. Nemeth
Tamara T. Butler
Grace D. Player

Published simultaneously by Teachers College Press,® 1234 Amsterdam Avenue, New York, NY 10027 and National Council of Teachers of English (NCTE), 340 N. Neil St., #104, Champaign, IL 61820.

Copyright © 2021 by Teachers College, Columbia University

Front cover design by Holly Grundon/BHG Graphics. Watercolor by Grace D. Player.

All paintings by Grace D. Player; all photographs by Emily A. Nemeth, Ashley Patterson, Bea Staley, and David Bwire

All rights reserved. No part of this publication may be reproduced or transmitted in any form or by any means, electronic or mechanical, including photocopy, or any information storage and retrieval system, without permission from the publisher. For reprint permission and other subsidiary rights requests, please contact Teachers College Press, Rights Dept.: tcpressrights@tc.columbia.edu.

Library of Congress Cataloging-in-Publication Data

Names: Kinloch, Valerie, 1974- editor.
Title: Where is the justice? Engaged pedagogies in schools and communities / Valerie
  Kinloch, Emily A. Nemeth, Tamara T. Butler, Grace D. Player.
Description: New York : Teachers College Press, [2021] | Series: Teaching for Social
  Justice   Series | Includes bibliographical references and index. | Summary:
  "This inspirational book is about engaged pedagogies, an approach to teaching
  and learning that centers dialogue, listening, equity, and connection among
  stakeholders who understand the human and ecological cost of inequality. The
  authors share their story of working with students, teachers, teacher educators,
  families, community members, and union leaders to create transformative practices
  within and beyond public school classrooms. This collaborative work occurred
  within various spaces-inside school buildings, libraries, churches, community
  gardens, nonprofit organizations, etc.-and afforded opportunities to grapple with
  engaged pedagogies in times of political crisis. Featuring descriptions from a district-
  wide initiative, this book offers practical and theoretical resources for educators
  wanting to center justice in their work with students. Through question-posing,
  color images, empirical observations, and use of scholarly and practitioner-driven
  literature, readers will learn how to use these resources to reconfigure schools and
  classrooms as sites of engagement for equity, justice, and love. Book Features:
Identifiers: LCCN 2021023597 (print) | LCCN 2021023598 (ebook) | ISBN
  9780807765999 (Paperback : acid-free paper) | ISBN 9780807766002 (Hardcover :
  acid-free paper) | ISBN 9780807779897 (eBook)
Subjects: LCSH: Critical pedagogy—United States. | Social justice and education—
  United States.
Classification: LCC LC196.5.U6 W48 2021 (print) | LCC LC196.5.U6 (ebook)
  | DDC 370.11/5—dc23
LC record available at https://lccn.loc.gov/2021023597
LC ebook record available at https://lccn.loc.gov/2021023598

Printed on acid-free paper
Manufactured in the United States of America

21 20 19 18 17 16 15 14   8 7 6 5 4 3 2 1

This book—
Its narratives,
Its call to action,
Its focus on justice,
and LOVE
Its commitment to equity—
is lovingly dedicated to
Eyatta Fischer
and to
Victoria Dunn.
You are both missed.
You are both remembered.
And you will always be loved.

Contents

Series Foreword   xi

Acknowledgments   xv

"For Justice": Our Found Poem #1

1. **Schools for What and for Whom? A Focus on Engaged Pedagogies**   1

   Engaged Pedagogy, Resistance, and Not Reform   3

   Trouble Behind and Ahead . . . Reform   8

   Pursuing Transformations   10

   Learning and Change   15

   Where Is the Justice? Overview   15

   Consider the Following   19

"On Not Waiting": Our Found Poem #2

2. **Bringing Learning to Life! Engaged Pedagogies in Practice**   23

   Coming Together: A BLTL Session at Connected   25

   Bringing Learning to . . . *What?* A Brief Overview   28

   Situating the Course in a Larger Context   32

   You Did What? An Overview of BLTL Projects   35

   BLTL Educator Pam Reed and a Focus on Positionality   37

   Engaged Pedagogies in Practice   39

What If?	40
Appendix 2.A: Examples of Other Course Texts and Readings	41
Appendix 2.B: Examples of BLTL Critical Service-Learning and Engagement Projects	42

"Waiting for . . .?": Our Found Poem #3

3. With a Revolutionary Mind: Literacies, Communities, and Engaged Pedagogies — **49**

A Brief Vignette	51
Hyphenating Literacies	53
Empathetic Leadership	60
Consider These: Reflective Prompts	65
Restoration	70

"Change, Changes, Changing": Our Found Poem #4

4. "Because I Am You": Engaged Pedagogies and Critical Youth Organizing Literacies — **75**

Time Travel	79
Imagination and the Impossible: Youth Futures	80
Establishing Context: Justice High School and BLTL	83
Reflections From the Wake: BLTL and the World Humanities Class	84
Engaging Activist Rhetorics: Cyberbullying and Neighborhood Pride	88
Ruptured Landscapes, Engaged Learning	91

"Being Radical": Our Found Poem #5

5. Where Is the Justice? Reconfiguring Time and Space for Engaged Pedagogies — **95**

Upheaval and Moments of Clarity	96
How Might These Things Look?	100

Civil Rights' Educators	100
Learningscapes: Setting the Stage	102
What About Time?	104
Reconfiguring Space as Place-Making	111
Expanded Learningscapes	115
The Paradoxes of Engaged Pedagogies	117
Improvisation Artists, Masterful Weavers	120

"Really Not Waiting": Our Found Poem #6

6. **Irradicable Impacts: Engaged Pedagogies as Invitations to Equitable Learningscapes** — **123**

Répondez S'il Vous Plaît: An Invitation	124
Scene I: Sisters' Organic Learningscapes	126
Scene II: Engaging Fraternal Proximities	128
Scene III: Engagement as Retention	131
Scene IV: Really . . . A Power Drill?	133
Scene V: An Invitation to Reclaim Our Futures	136

"Moving, Even in Stillness": Our Found Poem #7

7. **Waiting for What?** — **141**

This Is Not an Ending	144

"Waiting for What?" An Offering Found in Poetry (#8)

Notes — **153**

References — **157**

Index — **167**

About the Authors — **173**

Series Foreword

It's long been noted that justice is simply love expressed in the public square. And social justice? Justice, like love, is inherently social—there's no such thing as justice isolated from society, from human association, community, or collective.

Teaching for justice is at the heart of an education for free people. It's neither a fad nor a trend nor an add-on to "regular school." Rather, if freedom is the destination, justice is the pathway, and teaching, the guide. Social justice is the spirit of democracy made manifest.

Justice points to an educational ideal: the fullest development of each is the condition for the full development of all. Conversely, the fullest development of all is the condition for the full development of each.

Authentic learning, of course, requires free thought—curiosity, inquiry, problem-posing, question-asking—and assumes that students need no one's permission to interrogate the world. Learning is undermined when students are inspected, spied on, regulated, appraised, censured, measured, registered, counted, admonished, checked off, prevented, and sermonized, or, again, when they are read-off by their statistical profiles. Because these are the conventions in too many schools, thoughtful teachers must work hard to create their own classroom norms and fugitive spaces where students can exercise their natural agency and acknowledge their own true histories and deepest values, where justice is a question and a practice, and where glimpses of freedom are a regular feature.

We want schools that prepare free people to participate fully in a just society. We want schools that young people don't have to recover from. We want schools that act as the hopeful launchpads for the dreams of all of our youth.

Education is a fundamental human right and a basic social or community responsibility. Every child, simply by being born, has the right to a free, accessible, high-quality public education, which means that a decent, generously staffed school facility must be in easy reach for every family. This is not at all difficult to envision: What the most privileged parents have for their children right now—small class sizes, fully prepared and well-compensated teachers, physics and chemistry labs, sports teams, physical education, athletic fields and gymnasiums, after-school and summer programs, generous arts programs that include music, theater, and studio—is the baseline for what we want for all the children of our communities. Anything less weakens and then destroys democracy.

The curriculum must be forward-looking, recognizing the dignity of each person; strengthening tolerance, understanding, peace, and friendship among all people; and respecting fundamental freedoms and human rights. Schools must be geared toward the full development of the human mind and the human personality, which includes encouraging intellectual freedom and the ongoing consideration of these fundamental questions: Who are we? Where do we come from? What does this time require of us now? Where do we want to go? What do we owe one another?

Given the harsh, unresolved history of white supremacy and the adaptable and slippery nature of racial capitalism, it's no surprise that the descendants of enslaved workers, youth with African ancestors, the children of First Nations people, the laboring classes and immigrants from places devastated by our wars and extractions, and disabled and queer children too often experience schooling as oppressive and colonizing rather than liberating. This must change. Public schools can and must become sites of resistance, vigorously combating institutional racism, gender discrimination, ableism, and all other forms of oppression.

In your dream of dreams, what should a good school look like in a free and democratic and just society? What do schools need to do in order to fulfill the needs of free people with minds of their own? What could schools be, and what should they become, as fundamental pillars of a free society? Dare the schools build a just social order?

The authors of this energizing book, Valerie Kinloch, Emily Nemeth, Tamara Butler, and Grace D. Player, offer an emphatic, "Yes! Schools can and must be at the forefront of building a just social order!" Opening with love, gratitude, and an invitation to join the struggle for justice, these "researcher-educators" demonstrate their commitment to fostering and highlighting schools that are "intricately connected to equity, justice, freedom, and liberation" by sharing powerful examples from history—the Highlander Folk School, Citizenship Schools, and

Freedom Schools—and more recent contexts, including a community garden, a disability awareness campaign, and a high school English classroom. Punctuated with found poetry and pictures from classroom projects, laced with resources, and drawing on the authors' observational notes and interviews, each chapter provides a picture of teaching in action—complex, creative, and dynamic. Understanding that the best pedagogy is context-sensitive, no formulas are offered here; rather, the writers share their questions and underscore their alliances. The framework they highlight throughout is *engaged pedagogy*, or, in the words of bell hooks, "mutual participation" and the "practice of knowing together" as teachers and learners imagine and build the better future that we all deserve. We can do this, the book insists. Join in.

—William Ayers and Therese Quinn

Acknowledgments

We would like to recognize all the educators, young people, community leaders, and union organizers who were a part of the Bringing Learning to Life (BLTL) collaboration. Your energy, creativity, and visions for a better world are the essential components for justice-dreaming. You collectively embodied these qualities, and we are grateful for having had the chance to work alongside you for so many years. Our time together continues to offer us guidance in our own efforts as teachers, scholars, and community members committed to equity.

In addition, we acknowledge and thank the educators who so profoundly shaped the pedagogical learnings featured in this book. Your vibrant classrooms and centers were spaces where children and youth felt a sense of belonging, which made them sanctuaries for young people to think, read, dream, be, grieve, connect, love, act, make mistakes, recover, and create. Your network inside of schools and in community centers and neighborhood organizations is wide. Your knowledge, deeply informed by years of experience working with children and youth, is rich; your dialogues with families and community members is authentic, and your reflexivity around teaching practices is critical. You modeled what it looks like to root teaching and learning in love, trust, hope, and humility, with a sincere regard for and commitment to human dignity.

And for the students—some of whom are wrapping up high school, others who are now in classrooms of their own, some who are raising families, and many who are still in the struggle for justice—we thank you for inviting us into your lives and classrooms. You, too, continue to instruct us in *what* we write, *how* we write, *what* and *how* we teach, and in *how* we live.

To our biological and our chosen kin and friends: Thank you for being patient with us as we talked through ideas and vented through writing blocks. We are grateful for the time you made for us to write, create, and think, and for how you always encouraged us as we navigated the impact of a global pandemic and ongoing racial violence.

Thank you to the National Education Association and the Ohio Education Association; to Rhonda Johnson, Roberta Hantgan, donna Hicho, Tommy Ferguson, Brian Kellett, Kevin Kumashiro, Megan Brennan, Ashley Patterson, David Bwire, Bea Staley, and Brooke Harris Garad; and to our forever loved sista, Eyatta Fisher, whose time, efforts, and creative genius are woven into the very foundation of what made this book possible.

Finally, and equally important, to the community leaders, school leaders, and union organizers who insist on the centrality of the collective in movement building for justice, whose efforts rarely garnered the attention deserved, who modeled for us that the work is not about recognition, favors, or applause—it's about *the work*—we thank you.

"For Justice": Our Found Poem #1[1]

Offered by Valerie, Emily, Tamara, and Grace

Where is the justice
And what are we waiting for?
Engaged pedagogies *and*
Equity *and*
Justice work.
Not waiting for what?
Reform
That does not work
That does not center
The lives, literacies, joys, and realities
of
Black,
Latinx,
Indigenous,
and
Other People of Color.

We are in search of justice.

Will you join us?

CHAPTER 1

Schools for What and for Whom?
A Focus on Engaged Pedagogies

> When we all take risks, we participate mutually in the work of creating a learning community. . . . Expanding both heart and mind, engaged pedagogy makes us better learners because it asks us to embrace and explore the practice of knowing together. (bell hooks, 2010, pp. 21–22)

> The idea of freedom is inspiring. But what does it mean? (Angela Davis, 2008, n.p.)

Anti-Blackness.
High-stakes testing.
Criminalization of Black, Indigenous, Latinx,
and other Youth of Color.
Increasing school push-out rates of Black girls.
Overrepresentation of Black boys in special education classes.

The above realities are part of a long list, which also includes zero tolerance discipline policies, the school-to-prison pipeline, underfunded public schools, a lack of humanizing engagements and restorative justice for all students and teachers of color, a national refusal to combat and dismantle racism, ongoing disregard of structural inequalities endemic to U.S. society, and COVID-19. Collectively, these realities have become as much a part of schooling in the United States as antiquated report cards, attendance records, and classrooms with desks in straight rows. In fact, such realities make it difficult for us to imagine a time when schooling was intricately connected to equity, justice, freedom, and liberation.[2] As we see it, an ongoing challenge for many school administrators, boards, and systems is to make schooling for students, teachers, and families not about systematic maintenance (e.g., policing bodies, tracking students, demoralizing teachers, ridiculing families), but about collective futurity. That is, schooling must become a

Dreaming **by Grace D. Player**

site of justice in which our teaching and pedagogical engagements explicitly center creative problem-solving, radical imagination, freedom dreaming, restorative justice, equity, and activism.

As hooks (2010) implies, schooling, generally, and teaching, specifically, must encourage risk-taking if we are to "embrace and explore the practice of knowing together" (p. 22). It is this "knowing together" that is not punitive, that does not push out students, that rejects anti-Blackness, and that does not rely on zero tolerance discipline policies. Instead, this knowing represents an approach to engagement and engaged pedagogy that centers the multiple ways people "participate mutually in the work of creating a learning community" (p. 21).

In her discussion of engaged pedagogy, hooks (2010) emphasizes "mutual participation because it is the movement of ideas, exchanged by everyone, that forges a meaningful working relationship between everyone" (p. 21). For Black, Indigenous, Latinx, and other People of Color who are forced to live within a racist nation-state, we contend that engaged pedagogy must intentionally disrupt traditional systems of schooling that are guided by white,[3] middle-class, monolingual, and monocultural practices and deficit ideologies. **Engaged pedagogy** must see the whole person. **Engaged pedagogy** must emphasize linguistic and cultural pluralism. **Engaged pedagogy** must commit to racial justice and educational equity.

In fact, engaged pedagogy must view "the classroom [as] a place where wholeness is welcomed and students can be honest, even radically open. They can name their fears, voice their resistance to thinking, speak out, and they can also fully celebrate the moments where everything clicks and collective learning is taking place" (hooks, 2010, p. 21). Engaged pedagogy, then, must be grounded in equity, must be guided by questions of justice, and must lead to freedom.

ENGAGED PEDAGOGY, RESISTANCE, AND NOT REFORM

For us, hooks's (2010) engaged pedagogy raises important questions about schooling and schools such as: What are (or what must become) the purposes and functions of schooling? Can state-sanctioned schooling and schools positively cultivate, nourish, and nurture the lives and literacies of Black, Indigenous, Latinx, and other Students of Color without inflicting harm and without continuing to put many of them in a state of perpetual danger? How are schools addressing the violent legacies of colonialism, enslavement, erasure, genocide, and systems of oppression that continue to adversely impact Black, Indigenous, Latinx, and other People of Color? In what ways do schools address, or not address, those violent legacies *in classrooms* (e.g., through humanizing teaching, antiracist practices, and relevant learning), *through policies* (e.g., by hiring, paying, and retaining Teachers of Color), and *with communities* (e.g., through impactful, mutually beneficial collaborations)? How do we reconcile, to borrow the words of Alim and Paris (2018), that "in the United States and beyond, this saga of cultural and linguistic assault has had and continues to have devastating effects on the access, achievement, and well-being of students of color in public schools" (p. 1)? Are there alternatives to state-sanctioned schools and schooling?

YES, there are alternatives! **YES,** there are approaches that focus on learning and liberation and that emphasize engagement and justice:

> The Highlander Folk School is one example.
> The Citizenship Schools represent another example.
> And take a look at Freedom Schools.

Another concern that hooks's (2010) engaged pedagogy forces us to grapple with has to do with how schools and schooling criminalize Black, Indigenous, Latinx, and other Students of Color for performing resistance. For Kinloch (2017), performances of resistance often represent "a mode of communication or a particular, directed way of responding to the negative gaze, the degrading treatment, and the hurtful assumptions many youth of color receive from others, peers and adults alike" (p. 27). When enacted by Black students in educational spaces, these performances of resistance (e.g., eye-rolling, sharp verbal responses, silence, a seemingly disinterested disposition, absence) negatively mark them "as angry, hostile, and quasi-violent" (p. 27). Teachers, teacher educators, school administrators, and literacy researchers must recognize that many Black students and other Students of Color engage in these performances to

> protect and safeguard themselves from the harmful, potentially painful, damaging forms of interaction they often encounter from others who might misread, misunderstand, ridicule, and denigrate them. Given that schools are primary sites of ideological struggle—for racial and linguistic equality, for educational equity, against the criminalization and disenfranchisement of students of color—young people's performances of resistance are not uncommon. (p. 27)

In light of students' performances of resistance and the ongoing assault against their humanity, engaged pedagogy plays a significant role within the larger context of schooling and schools. In fact, it also plays a crucial role throughout society, as many Black people and other People of Color are painfully aware of the need to navigate systems of oppression, violence, inequities, and inequalities.

Throughout this book, we share examples of engaged pedagogy with students, teachers, teacher educators, and community partners who questioned the purposes of schooling and schools by identifying ways of "knowing together" (hooks, 2010, p. 22). The examples are framed by our collective commitment to reimagine schooling and rebuild schools by intentionally focusing on equity and justice. However, a subtext to our reimagining and rebuilding, named *educational policy reform*, quickly surfaced. This subtext forced us to pause and call into question whether educational policy reform and, more specifically, public school reform, departs from or continues to perpetuate structures and practices that are dehumanizing, oppressive, hateful, and xenophobic.

Note #1: We are aware that educational policy reform has a history of being
RACIST.

Reform in the United States has perpetuated structures
and practices steeped in
Anti-Blackness. Heteropatriarchy. Homophobia.
Sexism. Transphobia. Whiteness.
Capitalism. Oppression.

Note #2: We also agree with Bettina Love (2019) that
"the racist educational survival complex told dark families
that schools were 'separate but equal.'
More than a lie, it was a legal tactic to maintain
White superiority as Black folx
demanded to matter" (p. 28).[4]

Reform has been long seen as a necessary undertaking for educational and social institutions. However, the changing racial, ethnic, and linguistic demographics of the United States bring up this question: *Which* changes improve *whose* conditions, *for what* reasons, and at *what* costs? Whether schools are seen as brick-and-mortar structures, as a collection of computer codes and algorithms, or—we hope one day—as spaces that are humanizing, antiracist, loving, and transformative,

Mama Protester **by Grace D. Player**

we must recognize that it is the people teaching, learning, and doing *within* schools and *in* communities who galvanize change. Without their voices, lives, stories, documented experiences, activism, energy, leadership, teaching, and bold action, schools will continue to reproduce social inequality at the expense of the lives of Black, Indigenous, Latinx, and other People of Color. Schools will continue to be reformed into what they already are instead of what they can become. As we come to reimagine, refigure, and remake schools and schooling for children, young people, educators, administrators, families, and *for* and *with* communities, and as the title of this book indicates, we must ask ourselves the question: *Where Is the Justice?* And we can no longer answer that there is no justice or that we are waiting for justice to enter into decisions about reform. We must begin with justice as our guide.

It is also important to note that by reducing some of the most significant public school reforms to only acronyms (e.g., ESEA) and court case titles (e.g., *Lau v. Nichols*), the power, fight, sacrifices, and agency of the people who contribute(d) to WHAT we know about, HOW we think about, and the WAYS we come to do school become obscured. Frustrated parents in Topeka, Kansas, for instance, initiated what eventually led to *Brown v. Board of Education*, which overturned de facto segregation in schools. A concerned group of Chinese students and their families, whose stories are now woven into the historic Supreme Court case *Lau v. Nichols*, secured necessary resources for multilanguage learners to learn in classrooms across the United States. Relatedly, in *Gary B. v. Snyder*, children and families asserted their legal right to literacy and, more broadly, to an education.

A similar agentive spirit has long existed among teachers and their unions. In many of these collectives, teachers have pushed legislators to depart from dehumanizing practices of high-stakes testing and underfunding schools. In Seattle, Washington, teachers at Garfield High School boycotted the state's Measures of Academic Progress (MAP) test, compelling the superintendent to publicly acknowledge that the exam was not right for students. Years later, in 2016, in Detroit, Michigan, teachers successfully brought national attention to rodent-infested, dilapidated school buildings. They called upon the public to critically reflect on the question: Who, among our children, is forced to learn and play in such conditions, and why?

Fast forward to the year 2020. The U.S. 6th Circuit Court of Appeals ruled 2–1 that students attending public schools in Detroit, Michigan, have a right to "a basic minimum education." The suit exposed the harsh reality, among so many others, that students have been exposed to "classrooms where temperatures rose to above 90 or fell below freezing," that classrooms were infested with "mice, cockroaches, and other vermin regularly," and that "some classes had no teachers at all because of absences" (see Wisely, 2020a). For Detroit Mayor Mike Duggan, the ruling is significant because it proves what many of us already know—"Literacy is something every child should have a fair chance to attain" (see Wisely, 2020a; see also Mosley & McMahon, 2021).

> **Note #3:** Every child should have a right to more than a basic education.
> Yet we know that **not** all Children and Youth of Color in this country have been afforded the same right to an education as white children.

> **Note #4:** We also know that as we write this book, "the Republican-controlled Michigan Legislature has asked to intervene in the case, arguing that the court's ruling was infringing on its authority to regulate and to fund public education in Michigan.
> That request is being considered by the court." (Wisely, 2020b)

> **Note #5:** Septima Clark stated:
> "I want people to see children as human beings and not to think of the money that it costs nor to think of the amount of time that it will take, but to think of the lives that can be developed into Americans who will redeem the soul of America." (Clark & Brown, 1986, p. 121)

Like public school students, teachers, and teachers' unions, we are also aware that university students, professors, and staff have played pivotal roles in trying to reform education systems. In addition to preparing people for work within schools and communities, and conducting research that informs teaching and learning, many university teaching and teacher education scholars, for instance, have long declared their commitment to ensuring schools as safe harbors for intellectual, social, and personal growth. They have reimagined what it looks like and means for university classrooms to exist as sites of justice, equity, and engaged learning. According to Kinloch (2016), "for schools and colleges of education to be leaders in diversity, equity, and inclusion, they must heed Audre Lorde's (1984) advice to engage in a visible 'transformation of silence into language and action'" (n.a.). There are many critical and contemporary literacy scholars, on a long list of others, who take up this necessary work, including the following:

- April Baker-Bell (2020) in *Linguistic Justice: Black Language, Literacy, Identity, and Pedagogy*
- Maneka Deanna Brooks (2020) in *Transforming Literacy Education for Long-Term English Learners: Recognizing Brilliance in the Undervalued*
- Limarys Caraballo and Danny C. Martinez (2019) in "Leveraging Language(s): Reframing Rhetorics of Fear with Narratives of Agency and Hope"
- Alayna Eagle Shield, Django Paris, Rae Paris, and Timothy San Pedro (2020) in *Education in Movement Spaces: Standing Rock to Chicago Freedom Square*
- Jamila Lyiscott (2014) in "3 Ways to Speak English"
- Gholdy Muhammad (2020) in *Cultivating Genius: An Equity Framework for Culturally and Historically Responsive Literacy*
- Grace D. Player and Mónica González Ybarra (2021) in "Reimagining Literacy and Language Education for Girls of Color"
- Detra Price-Dennis (2019) in "'What Happens Here Can Change the World': Preparing Literacy Teachers in the Digital Age"

We take stock of what this transformation should look like through the sharing of humanizing visions of teaching and learning as framed by engaged pedagogy and because of justice. Thus, the subtext of educational reform with which we continue to wrestle will have to also be reframed by justice-driven engaged pedagogy and not by systematic maintenance.

TROUBLE BEHIND AND AHEAD . . . REFORM

We find ourselves in a troubling historic moment where private interest groups have managed to find a seat at the school reform table in order to, we contend, exploit public schools for profit. By conflating "learning with education" (Patel, 2016, p. 347), private interest groups focus on raising test scores and closing the achievement gap, rather than addressing and eliminating the education debt (Ladson-Billings, 2006) that is often insurmountable for many Students of Color from economically disenfranchised communities. Such conflations, according to Patel (2016), "partially explain how educational politicians have come to lead districts, nonprofit educational agencies, and schools of teacher education without having ever taught a day in the classroom themselves" (p. 347).

A contemporary example of this is the former U.S. Secretary of Education, Betsy DeVos, who has neither taught in nor led a public school or a college, and who is not a scholar-practitioner in literacy teaching and teacher education. DeVos is a proponent for school choice and a vocal advocate for charter schools in her home state of Michigan. As the founder of the Great Lakes Education Project, an education lobbying group, she helped Michigan become a state that "is generally free of caps" with regard to the number of charter schools and the number of students who enroll (National Alliance for Public Charter Schools [NAPC], 2015). In June 2016, the *New York Times* reported that for-profit companies "operate about 80 percent of charters in Michigan, far more than in any other state" (Zernike, 2016, para. 15). DeVos argued that school choice provides families with "freedom." However, she did not place attention on the hemorrhaging of public dollars out of public institutions or on the real issues of income stagnation, poverty, racism, and inadequate access to public transportation that many children and families encounter daily.

Now, more than ever, there is a need to attend to the discussion that seems to always unfold and refold around school reform. We need to critique the competing agendas of those committed to equitable schools for all children and those who are interested in promoting school choice for private gain. One of the ways we do this work is by understanding how children, youth, and teachers get positioned (by schools and through schooling) in the sociohistorical, economic, and political contexts in which their lives are situated. According to the National Education Policy Center report authored by Daniel et al. (2016), "part of the challenge in turning around schools is that outside-of-school factors likely account for twice as much of the variance in student outcomes as do inside-of-school factors" (p. 1). Stated differently, students rightfully bring into schools and classrooms their community, familial, cultural, economic, and social realities. Orfield (2014) rightfully observed the following:

> We thought race was a basic problem 50 years ago; now, in spite of abundant data on racial differences, we think we can safely ignore it and blame

communities of color for their own inequality. We blame the schools for falling behind our international competitors, none of which brings up so many of its children in poverty and isolation (UNICEF Innocenti Research Center, 2012) or sends such a large share of its youth to prison. (p. 275)

Race, however, has never been the problem. Racism and the racist systems that maintain educational inequities and social inequalities have been and continue to be the problems weighing against communities and People of Color in this country, and, according to Orfield, many people continue to falsely believe that "we can safely ignore it" (p. 275).

In the relentless face of racism, students "of African American, Latina/o, Indigenous American, Asian American, Pacific Islander American, and other longstanding and newcomer communities in our classrooms" (Paris, 2012, p. 94) continue to get up every day, time after time, and enter into school spaces—in person and/or virtually—only to suffer within "the educational survival complex" (Love, 2019, p. 17). It is unconscionable that we continue to tell them to be resilient and to accept and adapt to conditions that are steeped within systemic racial, economic, and linguistic injustices. Being resilient does not produce better schools. Being resilient does not address the persistence of racism embedded within racist structures and endured by countless People of Color. Being resilient does not eradicate racism. Being resilient does not guarantee freedom and justice.

Too much is at stake for us to only be reactive to whatever kind of reform DeVos had planned for our public schools. Any discussion about school reform must focus on school rebuilding in ways that foreground the actual lives and literacies of children, youth, and families alongside the harsh realities in which this country continuously tells people to be more "resilient," more "persistent," and more "tolerant." Resilience, persistence, and tolerance within racist, homophobic, transphobic, xenophobic, and inequitable educational and political systems have not and will never truly benefit communities and People of Color in this country. Just take a look at what happened on January 6, 2021, at the U.S. Capitol. So, again, we ask, *Where Is the Justice?*

PURSUING TRANSFORMATIONS

We (Valerie, Emily, Tamara, and Grace) acknowledge the complicated realities of, and racist attempts that work against, transforming schools into equitable, engaging places of learning for many children

Schools for What and for Whom? A Focus on Engaged Pedagogies

and young people in this country. Any attempt at transforming and improving schools must be done *with* students, teachers, families, and community members in ways that account for their agency and expertise, their safety and well-being, and their struggles and desires.[5] We attempt to do just that—to contextualize and share stories of learning and working *with* students, teachers, and community members, and, by extension, *with* families, school district representatives, and union leaders. Our working and learning *with* represents our ongoing uptake of engaged pedagogies and justice work with students inside schools that must get refigured into sites of learning, liberation, and love, and inside communities that must be understood as already existing sites of learning, liberation, and love.

Collaborating With

For more than 5 years, we collaborated with students, teachers, district representatives, and community members to galvanize resources across a midsize, midwestern city in the United States. This work was anchored in a city with a population of more than 850,000 and more than 10 degree-granting postsecondary institutions, including a large, public, research-intensive university. The partnering school district, which, at the time, was made up of 74 elementary schools, 22 middle schools, and 21 high schools, had a total enrollment of more than 50,000 students.

Collectively, we sought to explore teaching and learning as engaged pedagogies that could, in fact, lead to equity, justice, and freedom. As Hutton (2020) asserts, "The idea of freedom is inspiring. But what does it mean? If you are free in a political sense but have no food, what's that? The freedom to starve" (para. 8). Thus, we questioned meanings of freedom and for whom. We dreamed of schools as sites of freedom. We learned from freedom fighting students. We witnessed high school students learning about widespread hunger and poverty by partnering with volunteers at food pantries. We followed middle school students engaging in freedom learning by designing literacy projects with elementary students. And we watched elementary students collaborate with elders at a settlement house to learn about community, health, and care.

We wondered about freedom as connected to engaged pedagogy and justice. We listened to principals describe the urgency of teaching *with* students and not teaching scripted curricula. We learned about the unwavering advocacy of community organizations, families, and high school students to bring attention to and to end human trafficking. Doing these things *with* other people allowed us to lean into blurring boundaries between schools and communities, students and teachers, and students and researchers. We no longer wondered, *Where Is the Justice?* because we were actively working *with* and learning *from* others who were committed to producing necessary systems-level educational change in the name of justice. They were not reforming, but reimagining and rebuilding, refiguring and responding, which are directly connected to abolition.

Working With Others

The preposition "with" acknowledges distinct persons, but it also denotes a coming together, the formation of an "us." Our ambitious goal of being part of an engaging collective involving schools and communities could only have happened *with* teachers, students, families, community partners, and district and union representatives. We formed an alliance with the largest local teachers' union in the state and with one of the state's largest public school districts. Our alliance was directed by a collective desire to collaborate with students to focus on "the clear connection between their academic curriculum and real-world experience, while simultaneously strengthening students' engagement with school and the communities in which they live" (Buffenbarger, 2012, para. 7).

Through our collective desire, we became a community, or "a social unit composed of relationships, associations, practices, and networks of people with geographical, cultural, ideological, or some other defined connection" (Kinloch, 2009, p. 164). This definition firmly established and continues to inform our partnerships. Not only did teachers, teacher educators, students, families, community leaders, and researchers share the physical space of the city (e.g., mailing addresses and/or zip codes, city council, city ordinances, school levies), but we also shared a commitment to improving conditions within urban schools by engaging *with/in* communities.

Community also described the nature of our work and the learning opportunities that were created within and beyond schools. Initially, we turned to Lave and Wenger's (1991) conceptualization of communities of practice as a "set of relations among persons, activity, and world, over time and in relation with other tangential and overlapping communities of practice" (p. 98). In other words, "a community of practice is an intrinsic condition for the existence

Schools for What and for Whom? A Focus on Engaged Pedagogies

Stoop **by Grace D. Player**

of knowledge, not least because it provides the interpretive support necessary for making sense of its heritage" (p. 98). Through our explicit framing of engaged pedagogy for justice teaching and learning, we grappled with the concept of communities of practice (see Kinloch et al., 2015). Doing so pushed us to refigure the purposes of learning, participation, and partnerships as connected to the following overarching questions:

- What are engaged pedagogies?
- What do they look like inside schools and communities?
- How do we deepen the ways we become and remain a community?
- How do we admit to the ways we are not always functioning as a community, and what do we do about it?
- **Can schools be affirming spaces and engaging places? How?**
- As teachers and teacher educators, do we really engage with students?
- What do we really know about students?
- What do we know about the communities in which students live?
- What do students really know about us?
- Is our literacy work relevant with students and with/in communities?
- Is it relevant to our collective forms of learning and engaging, and to our justice work?
- **Could the work of engaged pedagogy get us closer to freedom and justice?**

Along with scholarship on and practices in engaged teaching and learning, these questions led us into conversations about equity and justice with one another and members of local communities.

With students, teachers, administrators, district and union representatives, and community agencies, we took an unwavering stance on the *what* and *how* of teaching and learning, which was different from school change driven by a top-down orientation. We understand teaching and learning as deeply social and participatory, and, as a result, susceptible to "temporary, productive failure" (Patel, 2016, p. 347; see also San Pedro & Kinloch, 2017). We welcomed opportunities to teach, learn, unlearn, relearn, and participate in learning by supporting pedagogical approaches that reinforced understandings of engaged pedagogy through school- and community-driven, critical service-learning projects. This work is informed by who we are as critical literacy and justice scholars, by who our collaborators are as freedom learners and freedom leaders, and by empirical studies and engagement practices that place communities' ways of knowing at the center of learning and social change.

LEARNING AND CHANGE

In their review of research on school change for the National Education Policy Center, Daniel et al. (2016) found that "improv[ing] student learning takes years of commitment by all stakeholders in the school," and they insist that "effective schools meaningfully engage families and the community" (p. 3). The coming together of these different groups of people (e.g., *all* stakeholders in schools and districts, families, and communities) provides additional support for students navigating schools and schooling experiences. It also recognizes the integral role of families, communities, and teachers in the lives and learning experiences of young people.

Kirp (2016) provides another example of the importance of collaborative school change. He examined two cases of school reform in New Jersey: the Newark City School system and the Union City School system. While the former opted for a "top-down approach" as well as "disruptive change, and charismatic leaders," or in other words, something done *to* schools, the latter "adopted the opposite approach, embracing the idea of gradual change and working within existing structures" (n.p.). Kirp found the approach within the Union City School system to be more successful, leading to increased graduation rates and the creation of new programs, including "Mandarin Chinese from preschool on, a STEM-focused elementary school and a nursery for young parents in high school" (para. 18). Innovating in schools *alongside* teachers protects their autonomy and rightfully centers their expertise and agency. We were, however, invested in knowing what "innovating" might look like as situated within engaged pedagogies, equity, and justice with teachers, students, *and* community members within and beyond the schools in which our collaborations occurred.

WHERE IS THE JUSTICE? OVERVIEW

Our focus on teaching, learning, and engagement within and beyond schools emphasizes the collaborative work of educators[6] from an urban school district, a local teachers' union, a land grant university, and community organizations who opened spaces, shared material resources, and designed community-engaged, critical service-learning projects. In so doing, we rely on critical and humanizing methodological approaches (Brayboy et al., 2012; Brown & Strega, 2005;

San Pedro & Kinloch, 2017; Torrez et al., 2019) that included the following:

> Dialogic listening and reciprocity;
> Visible commitments to self- and collective-determination;
> The formation of humanizing relationships;
> **Discourses of care, love, respect, and vulnerability;**
> Freedom learning and freedom leading; and
> **Enactments of justice and equity.**

We revisit data from participant interviews, conversational exchanges, classroom and community observations and visits, teaching journals, curricula plans, student-teacher-researcher field notes, demographics from the district, and reflection sessions. In addition, we engaged in data triangulation (Denzin & Lincoln, 2005; Kinloch et al., 2020). Overall, the collection of stories about engagement and justice that emerged from our data encourage us to push even harder for equitable educational opportunities, resources, time, and multiple learning spaces for students attending schools in urban districts. These stories also point to the critical need to refigure and rebuild schools, and not to simply reform them.

Each chapter in this book centers on specific teaching and learning experiences that are grounded in commitments to equity and justice, and that emphasize the valuable role of engaged pedagogies within school and community contexts. Additionally, each chapter focuses on the complexities related to the roles, methods, and perspectives that were shared among participants (students, teachers, researchers, families, and community partners). This collaborative work occurred within various spaces, from school buildings, libraries, and churches, to community gardens, food pantries, nonprofit organizations, and more. It afforded us opportunities to grapple with meanings of engaged pedagogies and equity.

An important feature of this book is its catalytic potential. Through verbal and artistic mappings, we reevaluate ideas, challenges, and questions that emerged from these engagements. We consider issues of sustainability, which get complicated by diminishing resources, mobility of participants, and the realistic exhaustion of teachers, students, and community partners committed to engaged pedagogies and justice work, but within educational systems of reform and not within systems that have been rebuilt. This is especially true during a global pandemic and continued racial violence.

Additionally, this text blends praxis with theory, metanarratives, illustrations, and the voices of collaborators. As a result, ***Where Is the Justice: Engaged Pedagogies in Schools and Communities*** serves as a resource for those who are invested in blurring institutional boundaries that artificially assign sole responsibility for educating children and young people and enacting social change within schools and communities.

In Chapter 2, "Bringing Learning to Life! Engaged Pedagogies in Practice," we focus on engaged pedagogies within various teaching and learning contexts. Attention is placed on the praxis nature of the Bringing Learning to Life (BLTL) initiative and the possibilities and challenges educators encountered with using engaged pedagogies. Then we contextualize how these pedagogies disrupt deficit narratives about engagement within urban schools and communities. Perspectives from BLTL educators and community partners push us to consider how engaged pedagogies can reframe public discourses about teaching/teachers and learning/learners, the role of freedom dreaming and freedom learning, and the significance of locating engaged pedagogies alongside commitments to equity and justice and in relation to stories about teaching and learning.

Chapter 3, "With a Revolutionary Mind: Literacies, Communities, and Engaged Pedagogies," explores literacy and engagement opportunities that emerged from two BLTL community-engaged projects (a community garden and a Disability Awareness Campaign) at Liberty High School. Central to our analyses are the learning stories of the Design Team, a group of students who engaged in strategic investigations at the hyphen—that is, the space between classrooms and neighborhoods, empathy and social change, and lived realities and redistributed power. These stories not only reflect some of the goals of engaged pedagogies and engaged learning but also redefine meanings of learning, leadership, and literacies within schools and communities. As we illustrate, the roles of students and teachers get refigured in ways that center equity within engaged pedagogies.

In Chapter 4, "'Because I Am You': Engaged Pedagogies and Critical Youth Organizing Literacies," we demonstrate how engaged pedagogies can generate collective forms of learning by emphasizing "critical youth organizing literacies" (Butler, 2017, p. 84). Reflecting on youth-orchestrated movements in support of Black lives mattering that have occurred across the country allows us to examine some of the equity, justice, and activist work that unfolded at Justice High School. We invite teachers and teacher educators to consider how classroom and community partnerships can foster activism, critical inquiry, and responsible engagements. In bearing witness to how young people define justice and engage in justice practices through protests, digital presentations, activism, and art, we better understand how classrooms can be refigured into spaces for critical teaching, learning, thinking, organizing, and engaging.

Chapter 5, "Where Is the Justice?: Reconfiguring Time and Space for Engaged Pedagogies," allows us to think broadly about engaged pedagogy, justice, time, and space. We dream and think aloud about ways educators refigured traditional spatial-temporal structures of schools to enrich the types of learning they made available to students and the kinds of social networks students could assemble to redress injustice. These spatial-temporal extensions of engaged pedagogies became foundational to *learningscapes*, that is, the relational places of learning where educators, students, and communities gathered to work toward equity—sometimes in concrete, visible ways, and other times in abstract, virtual, and symbolic ways. The stories featured here illustrate how traditional features of classrooms must change shape for new learning opportunities to emerge.

Chapter 6, "Irradicable Impacts: Engaged Pedagogies as Invitations to Equitable Learningscapes," explores the distinct ways siblings, classmates, and colleagues responded to BLTL's invitations to engage with one another. The invitations represent partial scenes and possible futures that unfolded in unforeseeable directions and intimate spaces that we could not access as researchers. These scenes challenge all who are committed to children, young people, educators, and the schools they enter to move beyond uniform, scalable impacts to include intimate and deeply personal encounters as valuable forms of engagement. Weaving these scenes together makes visible the scales of learning and justice-making and how they might be realized through unanticipated, unscripted connections. Illustrations of our collaboration underscore humanity as central to engaged pedagogies.

"Waiting for What?" is both our closing Chapter 7 title and an opening for continued conversations. In this chapter, we—a collective of women researchers-educators—turn to the criticality of poetry to think about larger lessons of justice teaching and learning. Poetry, as articulated by Ohito and Nyachae (2019), provides "a pathway for us to demonstrate rigor by (a) engendering precise identification, distilling, and conveying of evidence substantiating findings; (b) enriching researcher triangulation by prompting deepened dialogue—about and with data—to occur for coresearchers; and (c) stimulating reflexivity"

(p. 843). We offer a found poem as an artifact of our reflexivity—a collection of our ideas across and after the BLTL initiative that speaks to national realities in public education, generally, and in literacy education, specifically. We offer it here to "stimulate reflexivity" around our question, *Where Is the Justice?* and to encourage literacy educators, researchers, students, families, and communities to continue their efforts for equity and because of justice. Our found poem takes us full circle, as we underscore our argument that engaged pedagogies encourage the integration of

> The **lives** and **stories** of
> students, teachers, families, and community partners
> WITH
> The realities of the world in which we live.

Thus, there is a need to focus on equity and justice for those ready to ask *Where Is the Justice?* and ready to answer. Justice emerges in, and can only be sustained by, the deliberate centering of the engaged work that happens **with** teachers, students, families, and communities who are productively, lovingly, and intentionally changing schools and schooling.

CONSIDER THE FOLLOWING

Building on the legacy of students, teachers, families, teacher educators, and communities who have fortified the democratic relationship between schooling and education, we formed similar coalitions to refigure learning and rebuild schools across and within a public urban school district. The interinstitutional, intergenerational agency and expertise among collaborators proved to be powerful shaping forces in promoting an approach to teaching and learning that centered creative problem-solving, radical imagination, and restorative justice. We discuss the power of this work to shine a light on partnerships that exist in communities across the United States. The first steps in creating these partnerships begin with dialogue among people and a desire to repair segmentation between *public* schools and the *public.*

In the chapters that follow, we advocate for a shift in public consciousness to locate freedom and justice in education: freedom from dubious reform efforts of term-limited politicians, and justice to ensure that classrooms and schools are equitable places of learning, engaging, and inquiring. Before you enter the next chapter, we invite you to pause and consider the following questions:

- Do you have agency in how you teach and work with students?
- Do your students have agency in how they teach and learn?
- In your teaching, do you **collaborate** with community groups?
- How do you view engaged pedagogies in relation to teaching and learning as justice?
- How do you center students and communities in teaching and learning?
- What does it look like to have classroom discussions that critically examine questions of freedom and that enact creative practices in freedom with students?

"On Not Waiting": Our Found Poem #2

Offered by Valerie, Emily, Tamara, and Grace

Still waiting for what?
Engaged pedagogies and
Justice work.
Still waiting for what?
Bringing Learning to Life.
With students
With teachers
With Communities.
With and for us.

Because there is justice.

CHAPTER 2

Bringing Learning to Life!
Engaged Pedagogies in Practice

> All of those positive things about neighborhoods . . . (donna Hicho, community partner)
>
> Focus on what's best for students and teachers (Rhonda Johnson, former education director)

Her name is donna Hicho, with a lowercase "d," as she would always so sharply say with a look of inquisitiveness. She was executive director of Connected,[1] a nonprofit community development organization on the southside of the city that had as its primary responsibility sustainable collaborations with local residents. Seeking concrete ways to revitalize the community, Connected was clear about its commitment to the following five areas of investment: (1) Housing, (2) Business and economic development, (3) Community development, (4) Planning and coordination, and (5) Community safety and beautification. A major part of donna's work at Connected and a driving force of her activism and advocacy had everything to do with *partnering* with others to strengthen the community. In fact, she regularly sought out educational collaborations with teachers, students, and families, as well as district, community, and business leaders. She was committed to cocreating, codesigning, and co-implementing educational and community initiatives that emphasized learning, engagement, and equity. And as members of the Bringing Learning to Life (BLTL) initiative, we were inspired and mesmerized by her unflinching commitments.

donna's more than 25 years of activist and advocacy work within communities across the city and state influenced how BLTL educators, researchers, and partners came to understand the community surrounding Connected. In close proximity to Connected, there were, at the time of the BLTL initiative, four K–6 public schools that served as educational cornerstones in the community, and a 7–12 Science,

Kitchen Table **by Grace D. Player**

Technology, Engineering, and Mathematics (STEM) academy, a recently restructured high school that was once the community's heartbeat of civic life. In addition to a settlement house that partners with families in 12 zip codes in the surrounding community on child care as well as on youth, family, and community needs, there are also churches, day care centers, other nonprofit organizations, and a local housing authority. Over an extended period of time, the community underwent a significant population decline that was further exacerbated by the 2008 economic and housing crisis. Pair this reality with the spatial layout of the community, which occupies approximately 5.79 square miles in the northeastern part of this midwestern city. The community is only 3 miles from downtown, 2 miles from a major research-intensive university, and 6 miles from the city's international airport. Bounded on the east, west, and south by railroads operated by Conrail and divided by a major thoroughfare to the north and south, the roots of the community resulted from a land grant that President John Adams issued in 1800 to George Stevenson in recognition of his service in the American War of Independence.

Even with its interesting past and present, the community is more than these things combined. It is a place where residents are working to ensure a rich future that truly re-centers activism, arts, economic investment, and widespread community participation; where urban gardeners are intimately connecting with the land to produce healthy fruits and vegetables for families; and where collectives of people are creatively enacting new visions for teaching and learning. And on one Wednesday afternoon in late spring, some of these visions were on full display inside Connected.

COMING TOGETHER: A BLTL SESSION AT CONNECTED

The round clock on the wall of Connected's first-floor conference room struck 4:30 P.M. It was time for our BLTL class to start. On this particular day, 36 teachers and teacher educators, including Tamara (coauthor and former doctoral student-researcher), Doreen (a veteran public-school educator and community organizer), and Valerie (a university researcher and course instructor) gathered for our 2-hour BLTL session. Everyone in attendance was somehow connected to the local public school district and had committed to spending a 15-week semester together to focus on engaged pedagogies, critical service-learning, and justice work. As one of the three BLTL cohorts, or communities of practice (see Chapter 1), we were brought together by our collective investments in public education and desires to do our part to improve K–12 teaching and learning, especially in the city. During any given session, BLTL educators could be heard talking in small or large groups about their investments in the learning lives of children, youth, and families. For example, we overheard Pam Reed, a veteran middle school teacher, explaining to other educators: "I taught a lesson on decisionmaking because when we do our service-learning projects, the kids will have to provide service.... They need to know how to make decisions for themselves." On a different occasion and in the library of a middle school, Shawna Streeter, a veteran elementary school teacher, described how she always looks for ways to "make sure my kiddos get outside to play, learn and experiment, [and] explore together."

Pam and Shawna were not alone. From elementary teachers uncovering creative ways to teach reading and intentionally center Spanish language in the curricula, to middle school teachers designing and redesigning lessons on the harmful impact of bullying, to high school teachers learning with students about the dangers of human sex trafficking, BLTL educators were not just interested in refiguring the curricula. They were also invested in the role of engaged pedagogies and justice in collaborations with students, families, communities, and one another. They were having conversations and examining ways to address inequities and inequalities. They were collaborating with each other to not only imagine a better world but also write that world into existence. Their commitment to refiguring school(ing) and reimagining curricula surfaced in their uptake of learning as engagement and engagement as learning, which grounded our equity and justice work.

And then entered donna Hicho.

Initially, she stood in the back of the conference room listening to the framing of our class session, which focused on moving away from thinking about what critical service-learning projects *should* entail to collaborating with students, families, and community partners on designing, implementing, and evaluating community-engaged and community-focused initiatives. After we introduced her to BLTL educators, many of whom were already acquainted with her work at Connected, she came forward and opened with the following sentiments: "Many teachers working in our schools in this neighborhood don't know the neighborhood enough to help our young people develop a pride about where they come from and see that there is good in their neighborhood." She paused, took a quick survey of the room, acknowledged some familiar faces, and then continued:

> You know, all those words that you talked about [at the start of class]— diverse and developing and whatever.... My hope is that when you're in

a neighborhood, wherever it is, that eventually you see words like loving, vibrant, cultural, fun, noisy, crazy, loud, whatever. That you see beyond the missing pieces to what's really beneath and under there—spiritual, familiar, close knit. All of those positive things about neighborhoods that our media hides, that first impressions hide. It's just like meeting a person. You know, the first time you meet somebody, you judge just by the appearance on the outside. But after you get to know them, you learn so much more about their background and their history and their likes and their dislikes and their challenges and their loves. And it is the same way you need to approach a neighborhood like [this one] or any of the other neighborhoods that you might be working in.

donna's sentiments were just as much about knowing the neighborhoods in which we live and work as they were about collaborating *with*, listening *to*, and *seeing* people as agentive beings. We share her sentiments here because they encapsulate the type of engaged pedagogies we are committed to—the type that "see[s] beyond the missing pieces to what's really beneath and under there," or what donna also refers to as "spiritual, familiar, close knit." She pushes us to see, understand, and honor neighborhoods as collectives of people that include children and youth, adults and elders, families, organizers, teachers, and, among so many others, business, community, and education leaders. To use her words, we all play a vital role "in schools and in communities because we've gotta make a difference."

For the purposes of this chapter, donna Hicho's words are also fundamental to how we

> Designed and redesigned BLTL critical service-learning
> and community engagement courses;
> Enacted engaged pedagogies in teaching practices and learning
> experiences
> with BLTL K–12 educators and students;
> Witnessed and supported multiple engagement projects
> that resulted from this work; and
> Collectively committed to **"bringing learning to life."**

In the remainder of this chapter, we briefly describe the BLTL course and larger context, reference some of the projects that emerged from this initiative, turn the gaze on one of many projects curated by Pam Reed and her middle school students, and reflect on how engaged pedagogies in practice can, we believe, get us closer to addressing the following question: *Where is the justice?* We do these things from our grounding in equity and justice work. In subsequent chapters, we dive more deeply into answering this question by also thinking honestly about the subquestion: *What are we waiting for?* This allows us to further zero in on the specifics, dynamics, and significance of this work with some of the BLTL educators and students.

BRINGING LEARNING TO . . . *WHAT?* A BRIEF OVERVIEW

BLTL[2] was a grant-funded initiative with the National Education Association (NEA) that provided a tuition-free, three-credit-hour university course and other professional development opportunities in critical service-learning and community engagement to K–12 educators across a variety of areas. These areas included English language arts (ELA) and literacy, Spanish and language immersion, mathematics, science, technology, history and social studies, art, physical education and health, guidance counseling, social work, occupational and speech therapy, school nursing, and school leadership. Designed as a cohort experience, each BLTL educator (including us) committed to rethinking teaching and learning with students, families, and local organizations in ways that centered student engagement inside schools and within communities.

Class sessions, some of which occurred during the regular academic year and others during the summer months, were always mobile. Each week, we met at a different community site, including historical societies, settlement houses, community pride centers, a Jewish Community Center, food pantries, urban gardens, an Audubon center, the YMCA, the United Way, community schools, and universities. We learned alongside representatives from each site, who shared with us how their respective organization's mission, vision, and priorities were interwoven with the goals of the schools and communities with which they partnered. During our visit to a community pride center, for instance, many of us were awestruck by its explicit emphasis on learning as a means for "human survival," and we took this commitment back into our engaged practices. For weeks after our visit there, we continued to reflect aloud about reapproaching our teaching by always beginning with human survival as the learning objective. Because we were always in community and always writing about what we witnessed, how we felt, and how we were processing our

Bringing Learning to Life! Engaged Pedagogies in Practice

work as forms of engaged pedagogies and for justice, Valerie left that session and wrote the following:

> I continue to learn from amazing educators and advocates about how to not only survive, but thrive, and to do both in relation with others. It's that *with* and *for* others that fills me and that we always seem to start and end with in our work. . . . There's a collaborative spirit moving throughout this. A knowingness that this work is of . . . urgency. Intentionality. Change. It is about "human survival," and that will stay with me forever.

Throughout BLTL, we relied on the most recent edition of Kaye's (2010) *The Complete Guide to Service Learning: Proven, Practical Ways to Engage Students in Civic Responsibility, Academic Curriculum, & Social Action* as our mentor text because of its practical, hands-on framing of service-learning pedagogy. Just as importantly, we studied texts such as Collins's (1990) *Black Feminist Thought: Knowledge, Consciousness, and the Politics of Empowerment*; Maybach's (1996) "Investigating Urban Community Needs: Service Learning from a Social Justice Perspective"; Abravanel's (2003) "Building Community Through Service-Learning:

Ms. Washington and students from Liberty High, where Mr. Alston was principal

The Role of the Community Partner;" and others, in order to examine how we were entering into and participating in this work (see Appendix 2.A for a list of other texts, articles, and websites that were used in our course). The various texts that we relied on reminded us of our ongoing responsibilities to always consider and reconsider a number of questions such as these: What do "knowledge, consciousness, and the politics of empowerment" (to borrow Collins's [1990] words) mean and represent in justice-directed work? What does it require of us to meaningfully and lovingly see urban communities, generally, as rich texts that are layered with histories, memories, struggles, and joys that should be studied and elevated? What roles do educators—from students, classroom teachers, and administrators to families, caregivers, activists, and advocates—play in the work of engaged pedagogies in schools and communities? What does partnership really look like, involve, and imply? What does it mean to "Bring Learning to Life"?

During any given class session, BLTL educators, K–12 students, principals, and even community partners would find themselves gravitating to the front of the room to share something about their learning and emerging projects. From one educator saying, "I came across this essay. It reminded me of what we were discussing last week. Can I share it with y'all?" to another educator stating, "My high school students are here. They want to talk about their environmental science project," our learning was always a process of engagement. We were learning how to engage differently, openly, willingly, and vulnerably. We were asking questions and listening as we were also necessarily decentering ourselves in this process.

One evening, a group of high school students presented lessons they were learning in their English class about urban gardening and, more specifically, about forming relationships with others (see Chapter 3). They had their poster boards on display, and they distributed pamphlets they had designed. Then, the students explained how their critical service-learning and engagement project shaped their learning about the environment and created opportunities for them to work with each other in new ways. When they were finished, their principal, Mr. Alston, who indicated at the beginning of our class that he was "only passing through" and "could not stay," stood up and exclaimed that he "just couldn't leave." He went on to say, "You have to allow people to think outside the box because the larger picture, the greater picture here is: How will students be affected? Will they

Bringing Learning to Life! Engaged Pedagogies in Practice

want to be engaged? Will we improve relationships?" He continued by talking about the importance of building relationships with students:

> And those things, when you want to teach students, those things are more important than trying to, to stick to the curriculum. And we can probably go further in the curriculum if we establish the relationships, and we make sure students are engaged in what they're doing, and then we can find the connections to the curriculum . . . and students can get a much deeper understanding.

Mr. Alston's comment, "allow people to think outside the box," encapsulated the kind of work we were doing as a community of learners in BLTL. We were not only trying to create deeper "connections to the curriculum" but also seeking ways to think *with* students about what it means to "get a much deeper understanding" of engaged teaching and learning.

As a final course project, BLTL educators demonstrated different ways they sought to "get a much deeper understanding." They

A BLTL session

submitted mini proposals on an engagement and critical service-learning project they wanted to codesign and co-implement with students and community partners. Their project proposals were informed by many things, including their

- co-facilitation of the BLTL course;
- reflections on the readings;
- rejection of damaging terms such as "marginality," "on the fringes," and "underperforming";
- questions about what "not meeting adequate yearly progress" signifies;
- **interactions within community sites;**
- writings about practice and praxis;
- journal entries on the things they grappled with or conquered;
- observations of and discussions about presentations by other BLTL educators;
- **instances of learning from and listening to students**;
- streams of consciousness about, and uncertainties with, critical service-learning projects;
- small and large group interviews on equity and justice work;
- **feelings about giving up "control" of learning**;
- conference attendance and presentations;
- and, importantly, inquiries from students about how engagement with others could look, what it could mean, and what students, themselves, wanted to do differently.

SITUATING THE COURSE IN A LARGER CONTEXT

As we immersed ourselves in the BLTL course and debated intentional ways to enact engaged pedagogies in practice, the district was confronted with scandals about school personnel altering students' attendance records and changing their grades. These were done, allegedly, in an effort to impart an unrealistic, standardized, one-size-fits-all image of progress to district critics. It was not surprising that this accusation, which was investigated, was not situated within a larger discussion about the material and financial resources that are not always provided to urban schools. Shortly after the investigation, the district, along with the mayor's office, the teachers' union, social service organizations, elected officials, and clergy, collectively supported the bond issue and tax levy that came to be referred to as Issues 50 & 51. They argued that 50 & 51 would provide sorely needed funds to renovate school buildings, modernize technology, upgrade obsolete computer systems, finance preschool for all children, replicate high-performing schools in the district, and fund an independent auditor to examine district data and finances.

When election day came, Issues 50 & 51 failed, with 31% of the voters supporting it and 69% of the voters rejecting it. Regardless of where the voting population in the city stood on this bond issue and tax levy, one cannot deny the larger implications of underfunded public schools in many urban districts and communities. According to Rhonda Johnson, former president of the largest teachers' union in the state and recently retired director of education for the city, when 50 & 51 failed, "It [said] something about the failure to put at front and center urban teachers and students. It's a failure to address big issues staring at us. It's a failure to act because we're saying no to putting resources into eradicating big issues impacting us, especially students."

When asked, Rhonda said that some of those big issues include the following: "Hunger, health, socio-emotional needs, air-conditioned buildings where students aren't forced to learn **in classrooms that climb to 100 degrees** . . . functioning technology in schools, quality and available preschool for every kid." She concluded, "When we stop one-upping each other and focus on what's best for students and teachers, we can see clearly and work together to fill in the pieces that shouldn't be missing in the first place." Rhonda's directive about what we need to do—"stop one-upping each other," "see clearly," and "fill in the pieces"—echoes donna Hicho's plea to identify "positive things," "see words like loving, vibrant, cultural," and "see beyond the missing pieces." Their beliefs speak to the value of engaged pedagogies and learning opportunities that do not re-inscribe competitive, individualistic, and racist beliefs that benefit some and disadvantage others. And this is exactly what we took into our BLTL experiences with educators and students. There were, however, other events occurring in the nation during and immediately after the time of the BLTL course:

- *Barack H. Obama* was our president. The rapidity of problematic narratives proliferated about the United States being post-racial.
- *Freddie Gray* died of a spinal cord injury while in police custody in Baltimore, Maryland.
- *Sandra Bland* was stopped for a minor traffic violation and then found dead in a jail cell in Waller County, Texas.

Trayvon **by Grace D. Player**

- *Walter Scott* was killed by a police officer in North Charleston, South Carolina.
- *Miriam Carey* was killed by secret service and police officers in Washington, D.C.
- *Kimani Gray* was killed by plainclothes police officers in Brooklyn, New York.
- *Rekia Boyd* was shot in the head by a police detective in Chicago, Illinois.
- *Trayvon Benjamin Martin* was fatally shot by a private citizen in Sanford, Florida.

And there were many other events that impacted us and that continue to drive the work we do *with* others in schools and communities. These national tragedies (among many global tragedies too), paired with local scandals that confronted the district and the levies that were not passed, deepened our conversations about and commitments to equity, justice, freedom, and liberation. We knew that we had a responsibility to think with, learn from, and collaborate with BLTL educators. With them, we agreed that because of what was happening in the world, we would always

Listen to and learn from children, youth, and families.
Love students and nurture their creative pursuits.
Not get suffocated into believing that educational reform will work because it hasn't.
Work for educational rebuilding that centers the desires and needs of children, youth, families, educational practitioners, and community groups.
Outright reject deficit approaches.
Use humanizing, critical, anti-oppressive, anti-racist, equity-oriented practices.
"Put at front and center urban teachers and students," as Rhonda Johnson advised.
Commit to "bringing learning to life."

YOU DID WHAT? AN OVERVIEW OF BLTL PROJECTS

Over the course of BLTL, so many rich, layered, and engaging projects emerged and had a significant impact on people in various schools and communities throughout the city (see Appendix 2.A for examples of some of the many projects). In fact, some of the BLTL projects sought partnerships with Connected and donna Hicho, including the *Book Buddies Literacy and Mentoring* initiative that an elementary classroom designed and *A Better Us Composting and Recycling* project at the high school near Connected. The constant thread that ran through all the projects was the powerful image of connectivity, of "see[ing] beyond," and seeing "beneath and under there" that donna provided us.

At an elementary school only 10 minutes from Connected, BLTL educators Brenda Nieves-Ferguson and Michelle Fye partnered with 2nd-graders and initiated the project, *Latinos y CSIA: Construyendo Puentes de Salud* (Latinos and CSIA: Building Health Bridges). Students studied healthy habits, explored ways to take care of their bodies, and examined how nutrition and exercise can improve overall health. After they researched health issues experienced by some Latinx people in the city, they wrote an ABC health book with illustrations labeled in Spanish to inform other children about healthy habits. They donated their books to two local community organizations that served as partners on their project and that work with large populations of Latinx and Black residents.

In a different project, *Reading Mentors*, middle school guidance counselor and BLTL educator Erica Grimes, along with the school's Student Council and a Special Education Reading Group, partnered with a neighboring elementary school to implement a reading-mentoring-buddy program. As mentors, middle schoolers walked to the elementary school where they listened to, talked with, and mentored elementary-aged students. Across 2 academic years, they collectively focused on why literacy skills and practices are important, and the middle school students shared that they learned strategies for teaching reading while also learning to enhance their own literacy skills, voices, and leadership capacities.

Another example of a critical service-learning and community-engaged initiative is *Beyond the Black Berry Patch*, a project that involved a group of high school students who partnered with BLTL educator, Johnny Merry, and with local activists and community groups to research, collect, and analyze data on a historic African American neighborhood in the city—one that has been undergoing "revitalization" and experiencing gentrification. Students collected oral histories from current and past residents of the neighborhood, and published a journal that contains historical research, reflections, poems, visual art, and photographs about the area. They also learned how to interview residents, how to analyze interview data as texts, how to use Adobe InDesign publishing software, and how to engage in social justice efforts that could help to preserve the community.

And, yet another example is the *Cans for the Canopy: Kids, Cans, Conservation*, project that BLTL educator Antonia Mulvihill and her high school students designed. Students agreed that they wanted to learn about deforestation in an effort to prevent it in rural Rwanda. They raised funds to help Rwandan families purchase materials to make energy-efficient stoves that burn 80% less fuel. They collected aluminum cans to sell at a recycling center and donated the money to a local conservation group that purchases materials for the stoves for families in Rwanda. Their decisions were always driven by their dedication to using lessons they were learning about literacies and communities to address what they viewed as important environmental issues (e.g., deforestation, desertification) across the globe.

These BLTL projects and many others actively created "spaces for engagement" (Mulligan & Nadarajah, 2008) in which educators, students, and community partners freely asked questions, codesigned lessons, experimented with possible solutions, and relied on their engagements to experience teaching and learning together. Our work was framed by an understanding of community engagement that represents, according to the Carnegie Foundation, "collaboration between institutions of higher education and their larger communities (local, regional/state, national, global) for the mutually beneficial exchange of knowledge and resources in a context of partnership and reciprocity" (New England Resource Center, n.d.). We relied on this definition as we sought ways to connect with each other across our learning spaces—within schools, communities, and at the university.

BLTL EDUCATOR PAM REED AND A FOCUS ON POSITIONALITY

At the time of her participation in BLTL, Pam Reed was in her 12th year of teaching in the district. During one of our class sessions, she stood up, donning a large red t-shirt with the name of her middle school and an image of the school's mascot sprawled across the front, and shared: "So, the goal of the project is for them [students] to look at the grandest scale of bullying and to connect it to what they do every single day in the school." As soon as those words left her mouth, we could hear from other BLTL educators—

> Ahhhh and
> Ohhhh and
> **Wow** and
> That's good. I like that!

Pam described one of her critical service-learning projects, "Stand Up/Speak Out," as an effort to partner with students to learn about the dangers of being a bully or a bystander to bullying from a global perspective. Pam and her students agreed to explore connections between global atrocities of genocide, as a massive act of bullying, and the consequences of their own actions in school and the community. According to Pam, they wanted to learn about real-world, large-scale bullying and bystander incidents as a way to "connect what we know about self and service and how these work on a grand scale."

As Pam described the project, she also alluded to how she has evolved into a practitioner-scholar-activist by intentionally relying on engaged pedagogies to demonstrate how teaching, learning, and engaging must be based in experimentation, questioning, action, and reflection. In this way, engaged pedagogies are guided by commitments to equity, freedom, and justice that push us to think globally and act locally. When connected to critical service-learning, engaged pedagogies invite students, in Pam's words, to "totally have free rein on what the project itself is." Providing students with this freedom is necessary and, for Pam, supports students to examine issues such as genocide as well as the violence of marginalizing, discriminating against, and excluding people from society. In a journal entry, Pam described her investment in engaged pedagogies as a commitment to students. She wrote: "I love my students. I teach them. They teach me. We learn together, you know, we care about each other, 'cause that's how we learn [and] grow." Learning and growing together were key to all the projects that emerged from Pam's engaged pedagogies with students.

Elsewhere (Kinloch & Smagorinsky, 2014; Nemeth et al., 2014), we note that during an earlier group discussion about homelessness, class, and teacher positionality, Pam shared following:

> We [teachers] are going to learn way more than our students are going to learn . . . 'cause they live it, and we don't, most of us don't, and it's going to be more eye-opening for us than our kids, and if we could look at it

as not what we can give to our kids but what we can learn for ourselves, this is going to be a much more fruitful project.

This confession marked the beginning of Pam's "boundary crossing" in which she reflected on her experiences as a white, working-class woman who was venturing into an unfamiliar dialogic space. Over the next couple of months, Pam and her students began their search for answers to Greene's (1995) question: "What do we have to know, what do the schools have to teach to overcome divisiveness and group hostility?" (p. 172). Pam's students were always positioned as active learners, knowers, and doers who sought to both interrupt and eradicate injustices (e.g., bullying and genocide). Through her engaged pedagogies and because of her willingness to partner with students on critical service-learning and engaged projects, Pam provided openings within the curricula for students to explore, dialogue, reflect, and take action. Her middle school students were reading, writing, documenting, investigating, and proposing strategies for ending bullying on "a grand scale."

ENGAGED PEDAGOGIES IN PRACTICE

What if we actually do what donna Hicho asks us to do—that is, to *see* neighborhoods as "spiritual" and "familiar?" To *see* neighborhoods through the lens of love and care, where "close knit" relations thrive? What if we also commit to *seeing* neighborhoods as "site[s] of resistance," to borrow a phrase from bell hooks (1981, pp. 41–49), that nurture and nourish, prepare and protect people from harm, violence, and the unforgiving gaze of a racist world?

What if we *rebuild* schools into places, to use Rhonda Johnson's words, that "focus on what's best for students and teachers?" What if these are places that reject deficit perspectives and, instead, value, honor, and *see* students, teachers, families, and communities wholly and holistically; that center learning on the imaginings, wonderings, curiosities, and questions of children and young people; and that are steeped in transformative, critical service-learning projects?

What if we do these things through engaged pedagogies that push us to creatively refigure teaching, radically reimagine learning, and necessarily rebuild schools in transformative and equitable ways? What would this look like, and what would this require?

Teachers & Students **by Grace D. Player**

What if these types of engagements were at the heart of every student's schooling experiences? And, what if, in the larger context of BLTL, students and families had opportunities to respond to the bond issue and tax levy 50 & 51 before it was publicly rejected?

What if students were invited to design their own learning alongside their teachers?

What if students were asked to partner with their peers, teachers, and community representatives to design transformative learning experiences? What if they were encouraged to share their findings with school board members, superintendents, and community groups?

WHAT IF?

In the next chapter, we pause to share experiences with some of the aforementioned *what if* questions. We enter into an ELA classroom at Liberty High School and its partnering community sites to witness some of the many learning opportunities that emerged when students actively took the lead on two critical service-learning and community engaged projects: a community garden and a Disability

Awareness Campaign. As we enter, we ask you to consider some of our *what ifs* as you also reflect on the following practice-oriented questions:

- What roles do your students play inside classrooms?
- In what ways are you supporting students (and being supported yourselves) to design learning opportunities that rely on literacy practices to advocate for school and community change?
- How is your work representative of engaged pedagogies?
- What motivates you to keep doing this work?
- Where is the equity? The justice?
- **What are your "what ifs?"**

APPENDIX 2.A: EXAMPLES OF OTHER COURSE TEXTS AND READINGS

There were a variety of texts that we studied and discussed in BLTL and that we layered with a mix of other readings. We offer some of them here as reference:

- Adejumo's (2010) "Promoting artistic and cultural development through service learning and critical pedagogy in a low-income community art program"
- Calderón's (2007) *Race, poverty, and social justice: Multidisciplinary perspectives through service learning*
- Cammarota's (2011) "From hopelessness to hope: Social justice pedagogy in urban education and youth development"
- Greene's (1995) *Releasing the imagination: Essays on the arts, education, and social change*
- Hart's (2006) "Breaking literacy boundaries through critical service-learning: Education for the silenced and marginalized"
- Jordan's (2002) *Some of us did not die: New and selected essays of June Jordan*
- Ladson-Billings and Tate's (1995) "Toward a critical race theory of education"
- Mitchell's (2007) "Critical service-learning as social justice education: A case study of the citizen scholars program"
- Swaminathan's (2005) "Whose school is it anyway?" Student voices in an urban classroom

Other texts included websites such as the following:

- Campus Compact (https://compact.org)
- Children's Defense Fund (https://www.childrensdefense.org)
- Communities in Schools (http://www.communitiesinschools.org)
- Do Something (http://www.dosomething.org)
- National Network for Youth (http://www.nn4youth.org)
- National Service-Learning Clearinghouse (https://community-wealth.org/content/national-service-learning-clearinghouse)
- Stand for Children (http://stand.org)
- Soapbox—The Time is Now (https://www.youtube.com/watch?v=VVIAHarS1sQ)
- Youth Serve America (https://ysa.org)

APPENDIX 2.B: EXAMPLES OF BLTL CRITICAL SERVICE-LEARNING AND ENGAGEMENT PROJECTS

The following list represents only a small selection of critical service-learning and engagement projects from BLTL K–12 educators, students, and community partners.

Sample Elementary School Projects

Program: *Living Healthy*
Topics Addressed: Healthy lifestyles and collaborative learning with children and elders
Brief Description: In the community in which this elementary school is located, some students have been identified as having extremely high body mass index (BMI) statistics, which places them at risk for obesity. As part of the health and science curriculum, the prekindergarteners at the school study healthy lifestyles and question how they can influence others and lead through example. This project focuses on the following question: "How can students work with the local elderly community to promote and influence others to choose healthy lifestyles?" Participants learn about healthy living and engage in cross-generational interactions with community elders at a local community center. Each interaction focuses on a different Healthy Living

component that allows students and elders to study together and design and participate in hands-on activities.

Program: *Still I Rise*
Topics Addressed: Storytelling and educational choice
Brief Description: This project provides knowledge of Historically Black Colleges and Universities (HBCUs) and partners with students and educators to learn about the contributions HBCUs have made to society. Participants have agreed to research and learn about the histories of HBCUs and about their various academic offerings in order to think early about their postsecondary educational choices. Students consider career possibilities and the education needed for that particular career. The project's community partner, a local African and African American educational group, collaborates with students to learn how to integrate the principles of Ma'at and Nguzo Saba into their everyday lives and future goals. Mathematics, reading, writing, social studies, and research design methods are integrated into this project.

Program: *Book Buddies*
Topics Addressed: Literacy and mentoring
Brief Description: Third-grade students partner with 1st-grade reading buddies in order to expose 1st-grade students to a variety of reading texts; work with them to practice reading; provide them with books to take home; and to support 3rd-graders to learn to serve as mentors as they develop their own confidence, consciousness, and creativity with literacy and literary elements that they will then teach to 1st-graders. This partnership is especially beneficial for encouraging 3rd-graders to deepen their literacies and consider taking leadership roles in school. Students meet once a week with their buddy reader, and the books that all students receive will add to students' home reading libraries as well as reinforce the importance of reading in and beyond school.

Program: *Blankets for Babies*
Topics Addressed: Reading and community giving
Brief Description: Primary students are paired with 5th-graders who have had documented reports of engaging in bullying. They work together to break down some of the barriers and stereotypes that both groups have of each other. Then, they apply their lessons to a larger purpose: to make fleece tie blankets for a local children's hospital. The

learning goals for this project include participation in collaborative conversations about assumptions, identities, and needs; engagement with processes that involve mathematical problem solving, measurement, and calculations; involvement with the local community; and learning to question assumptions of others in order to work for a larger cause.

Program: *Bridging the Gap: Linking the Generations Through Service to All*
Topics Addressed: Healthy choices
Brief Description: This project engages students in learning about healthy food choices, gardening, and collaborating with a community of elders. Incorporating several different components, participants take part in a culminating project where elders and students work together to read about and examine the importance of healthy food choices, plant a community garden, and use the planted vegetables to feed the members of the school and local communities.

Sample Middle School Projects

Program: *I Can Empower Change*
Topics Addressed: Social change, art, community awareness
Brief Description: The goal of this project is for students to better understand that people have the ability to engage and lead change. This philosophy is established through work completed in tandem with residents who have chosen to live in a historically African American community in the city. The community's resident association committed to being the community partner. Participants discuss and present alongside students on the many different reasons they live in the community and what steps they are taking to ensure community preservation. This partnership connects to participants designing and creating community art (murals, street designs, etc.).

Program: *Community Art Service-Learning Lessons*
Topics Addressed: Community, art, homelessness, physical disabilities
Brief Description: A guiding goal of this engagement is for students to have leadership opportunities within their communities. Students take the lead on teaching art units to adults who are unable to fully care for themselves because of housing insecurities or physical disabilities. As a group, they share and collect each other's stories, understand sociopolitical and economic barriers, and examine new skills

in art media and creativity. They have opportunities to explore art as a way of expressing themselves, engaging in community with others, and as a possible interest and career path.

Program: *Recycled Urban Art*
Topics Addressed: Recycling and art
Brief Description: Participants gain an awareness of the costs of waste disposal. They learn that recycling municipal waste can offset disposal costs, and they gain an understanding of aluminum, a nonrenewable but recyclable resource they use every day. This project focuses on the resource economies of recycling aluminum cans as a way to develop understandings of one's impact on the amount of solid waste produced, and its impact on recycling, energy, and natural resources. As a result, students, teachers, and community groups read about, study, and then create recycled urban art that they share with others.

Program: *Integrating Nature*
Topics Addressed: Art and gardening
Project Description: Eighth-grade visual art students create art works, including drawings, poetry, garden sculptures, and paintings, for the school community. As they learn that many artists throughout history have been inspired by nature, they also examine ways to increase their literacy skills, document their literacy experiences, and exchange writings about literacy, art, and nature. Students decided to create two pieces of art to donate to the school community. They create a painting, drawing, or collage for the school's kitchen and cafeteria areas, where there are no windows. They also create a sculpture to be installed in the school's garden that another group of students will install. As a group, participants exchange ideas about, reflect on, and enhance their experiences with creating art works as they work at constructing an art piece to be donated to the local Children's Hospital.

Program: *Reading Mentors*
Topics Addressed: Reading and literacy
Project Description: The Student Council of a local middle school, along with a Special Education Reading Group, partnered with a neighborhood elementary school to implement a reading mentoring and buddy program. As reading mentors, students participate in an experience that allows them to read to elementary-aged students and reinforce to them crucial reading skills and practices that are integral to all 1st- and 2nd-grade elementary school students. Students learn how to "teach"

reading, how to collaborate with others to develop deeper reading skills, and how to improve their reading practices, skills, and engagements (guided by empathy) with others.

Sample High School Projects

Program: *Good Seeds Community Garden*
Topics Addressed: Community, collaboration, accessibility, and healthy foods
Brief Description: The Good Seeds Community Garden is the first wheelchair-accessible community flower and vegetable garden in this community. Originally created by the local church, the flower garden developed over the years into an engagement initiative for 9th-grade students attending a local high school. The project has evolved into a transdisciplinary critical service-learning project that incorporates English, science, technology, and art. Through the Design Team, a student-led group responsible for designing, coordinating, and implementing that effort, students develop leadership skills and participate in school-community collaborations.

Program: *Spanish FLEX (language experience mentoring project)*
Topics Addressed: Language and multicultural education
Brief Description: The goal of Spanish FLEX is for high school students to introduce Spanish to English-speaking elementary-aged students in order to codevelop a bilingual reading program. The project seeks to address cultural gaps between English-speaking and Spanish-speaking students by fostering critical, positive, and humanizing multicultural educational experiences grounded in language and culture. The agreed-upon goals include improving knowledge of Spanish and English vocabularies; honing writing and speaking skills; fostering a sense of community across Spanish, English, and bilingual speakers; and mentoring younger students.

Program: *Water, Water, Everywhere*
Topics Addressed: Water quality, clean environments
Brief Description: This project involves students in real-world hands-on investigations centered on water quality and how it is affected by improper disposal of hazardous materials. Students investigate the quality of the water supply in their local community, how the water supply can be contaminated, and what may contaminate it. The

project connects students to community-based organizations in order to foster ongoing critical service-learning and engagement activities around water quality and actions students can take to reduce and improve water contamination.

Program: *Campus-Wide Recycling*
Topics Addressed: Mathematics, research, and recycling
Brief Description: Students in an Integrated Algebra and Data Analysis (IADA) class researched and provided data to the school about recycling as a way to increase awareness to students, teachers, and administrators. Students worked with the National Honor Society to create a plan to implement recycling in the local school and to inform others about the various kinds of materials that are (and are not) recyclable. This work resulted in the creation of information, visuals, handouts, and lessons for classrooms and visitors to the campus.

Program: *A Better Us*
Topics Addressed: Mathematics, research, and recycling
Brief Description: This project focused on developing stronger emotional awareness in students and teachers, so they are able to understand and interact with other people as they learn to be in touch with their emotions. Participants focused on understanding the importance of caring for the environment, and they examined how their individual and collective actions affect the environment. Additionally, they created a green school environment with a usable composting and recycling system. In these ways, they sought to teach and learn with other students and educators in the building as they researched, developed, and shared a plan for creating a composting and recycling system with others within and outside the school. One of their hopes was to have their project serve as a potential model for other schools to design and implement.

"Waiting for . . . ?" Our Found Poem #3

Offered by Valerie, Emily, Tamara, and Grace

Waiting *for* what?
Waiting *on* what?
Engaged pedagogies and
Justice work.
With a revolutionary mind.
Through literacies
and
With communities.
Right now.

CHAPTER 3

With a Revolutionary Mind
Literacies, Communities, and Engaged Pedagogies

Scenes

Act I

Scene I: The Phone Call: A Brief Vignette
Scene II: The Design Team: Hyphenating Literacies

Act II

Scene I: Enter Jordan
Scene II: Empathetic Leadership
Scene III: Catalytic Empathy

Act III

Scene I: Restoration

Cast

9th-Grade ELA Teacher	Ms. Washington
Pastor 1	Paula
The Team	Angela, Benjamin, Brendan, Jordan, Sarah, Tanya, Victor, Brooke, Ruby, and Todd
Student with Revolutionary Mind	Jordan
Father	Jordan's Father
Brother	Jordan's Brother
Mentor	Jan
Principal	Mr. West
Pastor 2	Pastor Franks

Once students can imagine a range of possible worlds, they are better prepared to begin building the ones they want to see (Mirra, 2018, p. 5).

As another colleague succinctly stated, these 'others' whose lives we imagine don't want empathy, they want justice (Boler, 1999, p. 157).

In the following vignette, you will meet Ms. Washington, a 9th-grade English teacher at Liberty High School and an active collaborator in the Bringing Learning to Life (BLTL) initiative, along with her students and their community partner. The vignette provides context for the types of engaged pedagogies and learning opportunities that emerged from projects created in Ms. Washington's classroom. First is the organic formation of a community of practice of young people, across grades 9–12, that became a site for hyphenating literacies, leadership, and familial engagements. We understand hyphenating literacies as the piecing or bringing together of the multiple literacy identities, stances, and practices of people (e.g., students-as-scholars, students-as-agentive-beings in schools and communities, students-as-learners-as-teachers-as-ethnographers) within and across various geographies.

Ms. Washington and students brainstorming for Service-Learning Conference

The second is the role of empathy in this community, which is an oft-applauded, yet under-theorized dimension of engaged pedagogy. We discuss the prevalence of empathetic feelings in engaged pedagogies, their role in student learning, and, ultimately, how literacy educators can support students' critical reflections around this feeling by opening possibilities for self-exploration, coming clean at the hyphen, as Dimitriadis (2001, p. 578) put it, and justice-driven action.

These learning opportunities, among many others, rely on several design features of engaged pedagogies that include the following:

- Caring about students' lives, hopes, dreams, fears, and realities.
- Replacing systems of educational inequity with an education-as-justice movement.
- Repairing damaged and damaging relationships between schools and communities.
- Engaging in refiguring and rebuilding as a practice in abolitionism.
- Recognizing and leveraging spatial, material, and temporal affordances and human resources as restored through engagement.
- **Building an antiracist future.**
- Teaching justice.
- *Building with a revolutionary mind.*

A BRIEF VIGNETTE

As winter turned into spring and adolescent energies mirrored shifts in the seasons, or a kind of rebirth of life, Ms. Washington wanted to get her 9th-grade students outside.

"They need a morning recess," she insisted.

As if the world had been championing her inclinations, Paula, a local youth pastor at a church near the high school, contacted Ms. Washington to share that she welcomed direction with designing and planting a community garden. Several phone calls, texts messages, face-to-face meetings, and email exchanges later, a multiyear partnership was born out of their initial contact—one that addressed their complementary needs. Paula wanted to design a garden where neighborhood residents would come together, talk, and plant flowers and vegetables. Ms. Washington and her students wanted an outdoor space where they could run, rest, and engage. In fact, Ms. Washington also knew that being outside and inside the neighborhood would give students a kind of release that the four walls of her classroom, with one small window near the ceiling, could never provide.

A BLTL garden

Initially, the community garden was loosely tied to the 9th-grade English curriculum. Once students were immersed in the work of designing and planting the garden, Ms. Washington and her 9th-graders were quickly awakened to connections between the garden and their classroom. Students began asking questions about the kinds of flowers and vegetables that would grow best in the clay-like midwestern soil. They wondered about the types of plants that were invasive species and why knowing this even mattered. They also debated actions they could take to share their produce if they were successful with their planting. At multiple points in their planning process, they thought aloud about who would water the garden while they were on summer break. They were invested and curious in this new learning.

Ms. Washington nurtured students' curiosities by layering into the curriculum nonfiction readings about gardening. She scheduled additional time in the computer lab for them to search for answers to their pressing questions, jumping down rabbit holes of hyperlinks to articles and essays. She found *Seedfolks* by Paul Fleischman, a young adult novel about a group of neighbors from diverse backgrounds in Cleveland, Ohio, who came together to design their own community garden. She and her students read, analyzed, and discussed the novel.

It is here where our chapter picks up, between the rich, fertile (re)pairing of schools and neighborhoods, a space where community needs, state standards, and 9th-grade ELA curricula were sutured together and where bodies, practices, knowledges, and literacies congregated and converged. Some refer to this space as the hyphen (Fine, 2018; Jones & Jenkins, 2008), a reunification between schools and communities (Kinloch, 2009, 2010), a marker of "irreducible difference" (Jones & Jenkins, 2008, p. 480) yet an opportunity for relationships, connections, and serious reconsiderations of power relations. This is also a space to "potentiate possibilities unseen" (Fine, 2018, p. 10). Students in Ms. Washington's class understood this suturing together as natural. They grew stronger and more confident having their critical noticings, growing curiosities, and lived experiences seen, affirmed, and integrated into their schooling experiences and engagements with one another.

HYPHENATING LITERACIES

Out of the hyphenated space of engaged pedagogies flowed opportunities to read, write, investigate, question, draw meaningful connections, and, for many students, build relationships with peers that went beyond those intended by the design of traditional schools. As referenced in Chapter 2, we initially found Lave and Wenger's (1991) concept of communities of practice helpful in making sense of the Design Team, or Team, and its work (refer to Chapter 1). The Team was a small group of students who came together at Liberty High School around shared values, beliefs, and practices that explicitly focused on their humanity and that disregarded typical organizing forces of grade levels and academic "tracks."

> The Team rejected academic tracking.
> They said **NO** to tracking systems.
> They learned together
> by emphasizing **equity** and **engagement!**

The Team was composed of students who had participated in the community garden project their freshmen year; they remained connected by way of membership on the Team and by their shared engagements with reading, writing, thinking, and being. Apart from those who had just joined the Team as 9th-graders, the sophomores, juniors, and seniors neither received high school credit for participation on the Team nor were they required to participate. Yet they stuck with it. They built community with one another. They found purpose in their engagements and engaged work, which extended into deeper levels of purpose for their learning experiences. As reflected in the following passages, students broadened their visions of the interconnectedness of their present lives and futures.

"Our hearts are in this project," **Brooke** said.

For **Brendan**, "It made me want to just step ahead and just reach for a higher goal so I can become more successful and get out and explore and experience things. So, it opened up my mind more, like a lot."

For **Angela**, "I could help others, I could do something. I could really change something."

"Doing different projects" and "caring for one another" were important for **Benjamin**.

According to **Tanya**, the project "helped me look at things differently, at life differently."

Angela added, "I want to do well; I have to make sure that you do well too."

The Team skillfully navigated overlaps between school-based learning and community concerns. They were among the first students to notice, for instance, that the garden they had designed—with flower beds flush with the ground and a good 15-feet from the sidewalk—were inaccessible to some of the students at the school. The height and positioning of the beds prohibited anyone with mobility issues (7.3% of students at Liberty) from accessing the garden, a real concern for a school community that had one of two occupational handicap units in the district. Motivated to do something about it, students worked with Ms. Washington to evolve the project's focus and reshape its overall design. They wrote and received a small grant, secured additional in-kind labor from a local hardware store, and redesigned the garden to make it more accessible. They covered the muddy terrain in paver patio squares, raised the beds to wheelchair height, and placed a picnic table for resting weary spirits at the garden's edge.

The design of the garden was only part of the Team's concern. Their most impactful work was turning a critical gaze toward their own school and launching a Disability Awareness Campaign. They saw the Campaign as an opportunity to challenge ableism as it manifested in the layout of the school, the design of learning spaces, and in people's languages and behaviors. The building had significant design

We Do It for the Community **by Grace D. Player**

flaws, including foot-operated sinks in the bathrooms and inaccessible desks in many of the classrooms. Students had also observed and rejected deficit language about students with disabilities coming from the mouths of people at all levels of the school—from teachers and peers to administrators and visitors.

Embracing students' capacities for leadership, Ms. Washington explained, "For the kids that are a part of the Design Team, you know, they're leaders, and that wasn't even something that I was counting on. It just kind of happened." Although she did not anticipate the emergence of this group of student leaders, she nurtured their work and nourished their justice commitments. According to Ms. Washington, "I see, you know, in hindsight, how big of a piece that was for them. And for us in general. And now, I'm trying to make sure I keep that piece solid. Because it's huge."

The Team refined their skills of excavating sources of inequity. Powerful metaphors from the garden gave shape and offered strategies for equity work. *How do you get rid of a weed that thrives by crowding out and suffocating the life of other species?* You pull it out by the root.

> **Note**: The word radical comes
> from Latin *radic- radix*,
> which means "root."
> Rooting activities. Rooted action. Radical action!

First on the list—and there is no question that their work continued after our partnership ended—was ableism. Students created pamphlets for distribution in the school that talked about the importance of respecting body diversity and not underestimating people's capacities.

The Team competed in local rotary competitions to increase awareness and raise more money for their project, designing a trifold display board describing the history of the project, documented outcomes, and plans for the future. In addition, they presented at local and national conferences, creating PowerPoint slides and lists of talking points to guide their presentations. They solicited information from peers, "What did you do for your community?" and posted the written responses on cafeteria and hallway walls. With ease, students linked notorious school-based literacies with oft-forgotten community literacies by emphasizing approaches to reading, writing, speaking, listening, being in community, in family, and within shared cultural histories.

Leaders are often those people who see the bigger picture, who are able to make connections between seemingly disparate ideas. Leaders refuse to do things as usual just because that is the way things have always been done. They step out and step into the hyphen—in the space between what was and what can be—and they help others to see those potentialities.

And then entered Jordan.

"That was his idea," Ms. Washington said, explaining that Jordan, a 15-year-old African American boy at Liberty who was an active member of the Team, helped to coordinate a project fieldtrip to A Place to Be, an assisted-living facility for adults with critical-care needs. Jordan's father and brother worked there. His father had been there for more than 20 years; his brother was recently hired onto the staff. Jordan would often go with them to work to volunteer as needed.

Ms. Washington remembered that Jordan "told us about the place where he volunteered and we started talking about it, and next thing you know, we're getting a bus."

Taking a fieldtrip to A Place to Be was a pivotal moment not just for the project and the collective Team but also for Jordan. It (re)paired significant parts of his life: school, where he spent most of his day, and the Place, where he spent time with his father and brother, and had formed a relationship with Jan, a close mentor. Jordan talked to Jan about school, and Jan would share things he had learned about life with Jordan—invaluable exchanges afforded by intergenerational friendship. Jan taught Jordan how to drive. Jordan helped Jan with tasks around his apartment. Clearly, the promise of engaged pedagogies extended beyond the classroom and into community spaces.

Reshaping the project to include the professional lives of his father and brother created a new understanding of family engagement beyond the normative roles driven by white, middle-class values (Ishimaru et al., 2019). Jordan's father shared his social network with Ms. Washington and her students and, in so doing, enriched their collective experiences at the Place and their work on their projects. He was now seen as an educator who provided a critical source of knowledge to the 9th-grade English curriculum, to the focus of students' inquiries, and to the lives of students who were investigating topics of learning, engagement, accessibility, and ableism. In turn, family engagement looked differently for Ms. Washington and her students. It moved away from the unidirectional relationship of family members coming to school to "listen to" teachers and administrators *talk about* their kids to the school coming to the Place *to experience* engaged forms of learning.

Jordan's capacity for leadership was exposed, and Ms. Washington stepped in to offer support. Over time, Jordan drove significant movement within the project. Following the visit to A Place to Be, the project's focus shifted quickly toward a Disability Awareness Campaign at Liberty High School.

Immersing the entire class in A Place to Be, including members of the Team, created what Ellsworth (2004) described as pedagogy that is "dynamic," an approach to teaching and learning "that creates the *experience* of an idea, of a way of making sense of self, the world, and self in the world" (p. 38). Entering the Place, a space that was built to accommodate a diverse group of ideas and a variety of people, bodies, abilities, and ways of being, created irresolvable tensions with the garden. As a "community" garden intended to serve as a gathering space for neighborhood residents as well as for students and teachers at Liberty High, it had become, unintentionally, an exclusionary space.

Visiting the Place and understanding it as a space designed to accommodate diversely abled bodies, sharpened students' focus on the garden and their school, spaces that played host to some and that served as an obstacle course to others. Similar to the generative themes described by Freire (1970/2000) (e.g., discovering that one issue is connected to another, such as lack of transportation in a community as connected to high rates of missed doctor appointments, high rates of missed doctors' appointments as connected to poorer health within a community, etc.), students began to peel back the layers of limiting situations and barriers that inhibited the full humanity of their peers. Concrete realities that had been elusive to the perceptual grasp of some students, that had escaped naming and problem-posing, were coming into focus.

Jordan's acceleration in this pedagogical field of practice of community-engaged pedagogies became a distinctive space for him in comparison to the other spaces he navigated at Liberty, which he collapsed into an all-encompassing descriptor of "school." He regularly confessed, "I really hate school. I hate being here." Jordan especially hated his science class because he would get into tense exchanges with his teacher. He would either leave or get kicked out of science class every other day. Jordan shared, "I would just get up and get out and just go to the office or something. Go sit down somewhere else. And then that's what, that literally happened twice a week."

With a Revolutionary Mind: Literacies, Communities, and Engaged Pedagogies

Hallway **by Grace D. Player**

Leaving was an act of self-preservation for Jordan, but it was also an act that was unfairly documented on his academic transcript as incompetence. Jordan was not doing well in a class in which he actually had a very strong interest in the topic: science. At the time of our collaboration, Jordan was piecing together his sophomore year schedule, and he was considering which AP courses he should take to prepare for college.

Interested in advanced coursework yet existing on the margins of 9th-grade science—having to hang out in the "office or something"—Jordan sought refuge, nurtured his curiosities, and strengthened his relationship with "school." He did these things because of the power of Ms. Washington's engaged pedagogies and because of the engaged projects she included in class. On one of the days Jordan was planning to stay home from school because he did not want to go, he received a text from Ms. Washington. He explained, "And I was just going through my text messages. Seen Ms. Washington's text message, 'oh yeah yeah, I'm going to this class.' So I threw something on." Jordan was flirting with a truancy charge, but that was not his source of motivation for going to school that day. He went to school because he knew Ms. Washington's rule: If he wasn't in class, he risked not being able to participate in and engage with the project.

Repairing fractured relationships that exist among schools, communities, and familial engagements, as represented by the community garden project and the Disability Awareness Campaign, encouraged Jordan to see himself as fully capable of doing school the way he wanted to do school. It also reinforced relationships between thought and action. On many separate occasions, Ms. Washington described Jordan as "my thinker" and as someone who "needs to be doing." Repairing the body and the mind is essential to engaged work. Jordan was freed up to lead, stepping up and into justice spaces where he and his classmates could creatively problem-pose and problem-solve by drawing on stories, literary elements, diverse genres of writing, dialogue, movement, and critical reading skills within purpose-driven, meaningful relationships. This was a significant materialization of engaged pedagogies and engaged learning.

The Team reinforced a newfound purpose of school as a site in which deep, meaningful, and engaged forms of learning could actually be felt, embodied, and experienced. This reassertion that school is a hub of educational pursuits rather than that which contains or constrains an education by way of external, private, neoliberal forces (Au, 2016), supports young people and teachers to be generative in their learning opportunities. In this case, learning was born out of, and became strengthened because of, the hyphen between school and community. Open to these possibilities, the Team challenged the notion that their identities are reduced to the title of student within the context of school. Establishing school as a *context* for educational endeavors, not the container, allowed students to journey, create, experiment with, and (re)design learning opportunities out of which responsibilities and relationships emerged (Kinloch et al., 2015; Nemeth & Winterbottom, 2016; Reed & Butler, 2014).

EMPATHETIC LEADERSHIP

The projects in Ms. Washington's class reinforced the cultivation of critical leadership skills and social change strategies. They represented an extension, or a critical expansion, of the English curriculum for students who sought additional ways to connect lessons learned from classroom texts with engagements steeped in meaning-making modes and problem-posing strategies about encounters faced in public life. For Jordan and other Black youth navigating the institution of school—a site that can feel dehumanizing (for Jordan) and filled with spirit-murdering tactics (Love, 2019)—community-engaged approaches to teaching and learning offered a respite for students being pushed out (Morris, 2018). Such approaches also helped to fundamentally change students' relationships and interactions with peers, especially as they learned to assert their identities, embrace their literacies, and individually and collectively "take their place intelligently in a changing world" (Horton et al., 1998, p. 56).

Taking One's Place: An Example From the Highlander Folk School

What does it look like to take one's place intelligently in the world, as educator Myles Horton urged visitors to do at the Highlander Folk School? For Horton, who, in 1932, cofounded the school with educator Don West and minister James A. Dombrowski in Grundy County, Tennessee, it meant trusting that everyone has the capacity to govern themselves, to ask questions, to use their experiences to make sense of the world, and to create integrated spaces for people to gather, talk, learn, and strategize. It goes without saying that the Highlander Folk School (now known as the Highlander Research and Education Center, located in New Market, Tennessee) has a rich legacy of leadership for social change and a powerful history of engaging in movements that connect education with human rights. For example, the school and its leaders were involved in labor rights movements in the 1930s and the Citizenship School movement in the 1950s. Rights leaders, activists, and educators, including Septima Clark, Rosa Parks, Martin Luther King Jr., Anne Braden, Ralph Abernathy, John Lewis, Bernice Robinson, and Esau Jenkins, among others, either received early training from or partnered with the school to advocate for the civil, economic, educational, political, and social rights of people disenfranchised and disregarded by a racist society.

The reservoir of knowledge about leadership for social change is deep within the history of Highlander and within social movements such as the Citizenship Schools in the South. One powerful learning that has application in schools and within these emergent communities of practice is the idea of "yeasty education," that is, an education "that will multiply itself," and educators who "have the potential to multiply themselves and fundamentally change society" (Horton et al., 1998, p. 57).

At Liberty High School, members of the Team, especially Jordan, grew increasingly frustrated that the Team's ideas had not caught on in the yeasty kind of way that can productively impact communities.

Jordan lamented, "I think people don't even care, I think they're just going to be like, 'oh that's sad, that's crazy' and then go back to eating their dinner." Jordan, skillful at intertextuality and mindful of the valuable role of the arts in helping us to understand human conditions, was drawing on the film, *Hotel Rwanda*, based on the *actual* genocide of the Tutsi people. He was referring to a particular exchange between the hotel manager, Paul Rusesabagina (Don Cheadle), who was sheltering refugees from genocide, and a member the U.S. press, Jack Daglish (Joaquin Phoenix). In this scene, Rusesabagina expressed gratitude that Daglish had captured video of the genocide and was going to air the footage in the United States:

Rusesabagina: "I'm glad that you have showed this footage and that the world will see it. It is the only way we have a chance that people might intervene."
Daglish countered: "Yeah, if no one intervenes, is it still a good thing to show?"
Rusesabagina questioned: "How can they not intervene when they witness such atrocities?"
Daglish responded: [the energy in his voice dulled] "Aww, I think if people see this footage, they'll say 'oh my God, that's horrible,' and go on eating their dinners."

Jordan likened the behaviors of his peers to those of the U.S. citizens who went on "eating their dinner": "That's exactly how I think people act like this. Like, say some people do this when they have freshman year with Ms. Washington, and they be all into it and everything. Sophomore year comes, they just stop doing it." He went on to share, "They do it because they, they basically have to because Ms. Washington goes out there anyways. And then, *some* get it."

When Jordan paused, we inquired, "They stopped doing it because they didn't have to do it?" Jordan's response: "Yeah. So they just kind of went back to . . . being their selves." Some of his classmates, Jordan argued, had stopped participating, defaulting to what he described as a disengaged self.

Of the hours of interview data and pages of transcription notes from Ms. Washington's classroom, the sharing of this exchange with Jordan has stuck with us. Jordan was highlighting one of the shortcomings of engaged pedagogies and the reality that *"some* students get it" and others don't. Or maybe it's more complex. To "get it" means something different for everyone. Some students personalize, internalize, and feel for another person, but might not yet see the systemic nature of the problem and their role in alleviating human suffering in tangible ways. Some go even further—break free of the bounds of their classroom walls and grade bands—to participate, to become, and to build a community around the practice, like members of the Team.

Jordan contrasted himself with his peers: They had remained "their selves," to use his words, whereas he had in fact changed. The Disability Campaign had become an extension of his values, and he became an extension of the Campaign.

Additionally, Jordan reminds us that we cannot assume that students will immediately get it and will get involved. As literacy educators, we understand and grapple with Jordan's point that ideas and, in this case, exposing an ideology such as ableism, making sense of it, and then challenging it, do not land with all of our students or with some of us the very first time. We also know this happens for a number of reasons and that responsibility to try to make sense of an idea, to expose and grapple with an ideology, rests with each of us, educators and students, across the short- and long-term. Fortunate for us, there is often an opportunity to try again—and again. While we acknowledge the many beliefs pressing down on K–12 schools, from a neoliberal framework, that learning should somehow be businesslike, efficient, ever-forward moving, and exact, we know that these beliefs are problematic and that they require the opposite: They are time-intensive, iterative, and messy. Toward that end, we believe that Jordan was offering us more than a clue about where we might begin to try again within teaching and learning as engaged pedagogies—that is, with empathy.

Leaning Into and Learning From Empathy

Empathy is an inescapable dimension of engaged pedagogies that can result from human encounter, but it is sometimes discussed as an "unmitigated good" (Langstraat & Bowdon, 2011), an example of the "remainders" (Butin, 2003) that surface through engaged learning. Yet it does not often get integrated into classroom discussions about learning. Langstraat and Bowdon (2011) insist that emotions in service-learning literature, for instance, woefully undertheorized empathy, and, when addressed, discussions are done so implicitly. Jordan plucked this issue right out of the center of this scholarly debate.

In her call for moving beyond empathy in service-learning, a form of community-engaged pedagogy, Rosenberger (2000) exposed the superficial levels of engagement of some service learners who merely feel bad for the people they are "helping," whose engagements with *others* are fraught with unexamined assumptions and naïve consciousnesses about power, privilege, and inequity. Rosenberger's (2000) call can be applied to engaged pedagogies more generally because, like service-learning, they promote human encounters. Similarly, Bowdon et al. (2014) expose empathy as an unquestioned ideal outcome of service-learning, insisting that empathy instead should be seen as "a complicated and unstable element that is constantly shaped by a number of factors, including individual, social, and cultural histories and contexts" (p. 58). The minimizing and essentializing that can result from empathy gone wrong (p. 58) motivated Bowdon and coauthors to isolate empathetic desires as sites of analysis, including those already part of service-learning and service-learners at the beginning of involvement. They promote a "practiced 'feminist' affective ethic that encourages students to serve others toward the ends of social justice and the collective good" (p. 59). If left unaddressed, unquestioned, and decontextualized, students can cultivate what Boler (1999) calls passive empathy, missing an opportunity to interrogate "one's complicit responsibility within historical and social conditions" (p. 164).

Boler (1999) points out that passive empathetic reading of traditional alphabetic texts happens all the time and is "founded on a binary of self/other that situates the self/reader unproblematically as judge" (p. 160). She writes, "This self is not required to identify with the oppressor, and not required to identify her complicity in structures of power relations mirrored by the text" (p. 160). While the reader, in this case, is not a participant in the unfolding narrative of the text, the reader could very well be implicated in the injustices relayed by the characters and plot as they exist in analogous forms out in the physical, social world. Lacking a reflexive practice, the reader might feel sadness on behalf of a character but is freed from doing the difficult work of self-interrogation.

Not all of us venture into a text looking for ways we are implicated in human suffering. This might not only be intentional distancing work on our part, but rather a default orientation for a reader who is reading for pleasure. As Wolf (2018) writes about empathetic readings in literature, "we welcome the Other. For a moment in time, we leave ourselves; and when we return, sometimes expanded and strengthened, we are changed both intellectually and emotionally" (p. 44). One is able "to leave and yet not leave one's sphere" (p. 43). We think what Jordan was pointing out is that empathy, left alone, without requisite reflective prompts, might be mere consumption rather than the intellectual shifts suggested by Wolf.

CONSIDER THESE: REFLECTIVE PROMPTS

- If you could give our project a title, what would you call it?
- How would you describe the goal of our work with/in the community?
- What do you think we hope to achieve?
- Draw an image or a Venn diagram that **captures overlaps** between your life and the life/lives of the person/people with whom we're partnering. Where are there similarities? Where are there differences?
- Which of the following best captures your feelings toward our work with/in the community? Feel free to circle more than one. Then consider **specific stories connected with** any of the feelings.
    - » Accepting/open
    - » Aliveness/joy
    - » Angry/annoyed
    - » Courageous/powerful
    - » Connected/loving
    - » Curious
    - » Despair/sad
    - » Disconnected/numb
    - » Embarrassed/shame
    - » Fragile/grateful
    - » Guilt
    - » Hopeful
    - » Powerless
    - » Stressed/tense
    - » Unsettled/doubt

We are not suggesting that schooling and, more specifically, education, should *make* students *feel* a particular way (other than loved and human!). We are, however, arguing that empathy is not an "unmitigated good" (Langstraat & Bowdon, 2011, p.8) and that we are wise to think of ways to encourage students to identify this feeling, think about its origin, and grapple with what to do with such a feeling (how to engage it). As Lauren Olamina, Butler's (1993) fictional heroine in *Parable of the Sower* demonstrates, empathy can hold us captive in an emotional state or move us toward intelligent action.

Catalytic Empathy

Jordan moved us toward theorizing a kind of catalytic empathy (Nemeth, 2017), a movement toward action emerging from a place of felt responsibility. We initially turned to the work of Boler (1999) who explored empathy in the context of reading to argue for a "testimonial reading" that "involves empathy, but requires the reader's responsibility" (pp. 157–158). She contends, "ideally, testimonial reading inspires an empathetic response that motivates action: a 'historicized ethics' engaged across genres, that radically shifts our self-reflective understanding of power relations" (p. 158). Ellsworth's (2004) notion of labor of response and Mirra's (2018) more recent critical civic empathy also informed our understandings of catalytic empathy within engaged pedagogies.

For Ellsworth (2004), labor of response is embedded in spaces of learning—not necessarily classrooms—rather what she calls anomalous places, such as poems, art, memorials, artifacts, bodies by way of museums, film, media, and staged performances, which become educative. She argued that these become sites of emergent selves, learning selves, and changed selves. She refers to the Holocaust Museum to illustrate her point, calling it a "pedagogical masterpiece" (p. 113), one that refrains from categorizing visitors as "victim, perpetrator, bystander, rescuer, or liberator of the Holocaust" (p. 113) and instead, creates a "condition of responsibility" (p. 113) for all by inviting labor of response. Ellsworth argues that "this labor of response can only take place in the space of difference between the self who is held hostage to an imperative and the self who is free to step out into the daylight" (p. 112). Someone who has taken the imperative seriously might physically leave the museum, and yet the museum experience is now part of the mind and is grappling with tension of (in)action.

Along with Ellsworth's thinking, Boler (1999) reminds us that it is not the case that understanding something leads to responsibility. Instead, the goal is to stage responsibility—to create a predicament, a tension, to illuminate the imperative within the learning opportunity. Educators at Highlander Folk School, for example, believed the same: Support people to be in a position to act on their espoused values (Horton et al., 1998). Staging responsibility in engaged pedagogies releases teachers from the potentially unachievable, even unethical, task of *making* students particular kinds of people. Staging, instead, suggests creating or designing "transitional spaces" (p. 17) for learning where opportunities for change—of intellect and emotion, as suggested by Wolf (2018), and ways of being in the world, as promoted by Highlander and the legacy of leaders within social movements—are made possible.

Jordan leveraged the scene in *Hotel Rwanda* to illustrate the consequences of passivity, inaction, and perhaps the limits of empathy. Also embedded in his reflections is a belief in the promise of everyday people acting, doing, and leading. Thus, we are left to deeply consider what this means for engaged pedagogies and the people who employ them.

As Boler (1999) reminds us, "in question is not the text itself, but what reading practices are taught, and how such texts function within educational objectives" (pp. 157–158). She *encourages* educators to *encourage* students to participate in "testimonial readings," which involve "empathy, but requires the reader's responsibility" (pp. 157–158). To talk openly about a reader's responsibility in a character's plight is to simultaneously create opportunities for investigation of cultural, structural, and interpersonal manifestations of oppression. Catalytic forms of empathetic readings of the world and of human encounters within engaged pedagogies, then, can also lead to opportunities for critical understandings of social issues under investigation. Catalytic empathy helps to manage the pitfall of engaged pedagogies and practices that fall into binary positionings of students and community partners, or students versus community partners (Patterson et al., 2017). It recognizes that the hyphen between school and community, and between self and another, signifies an "irreducible difference" (Jones & Jenkins, 2008, p. 480).

Being Open

What would it look like to be open to all subject positions relative to the problem being relayed in a text or the problem being textualized (Bloome & Egan-Robertson, 1993) by students within engaged pedagogies and by engaged projects? We believe that it is important to be open with students about the potentialities of engaged pedagogies, which include the emergence of emotions, such as empathy, and how to manage them. For example, engaged pedagogies must encourage students to move beyond an often-passive sense of sympathy or pity that dislocates people and social issues from sociocultural, historicized, familial, and/or economic contexts. Instead, a major promise of engaged pedagogies is that it can establish deeper connections of people and issues to empathy and compassion, or to what Boler (1999) describes as *feeling with*, only if, as we contend, this *feeling with* is rooted in equity, ethics, and justice. As Langstraat and Bowdon (2011) write, "helping students distinguish among sympathy, pity, empathy, and compassion is vital, particularly insofar as it leads to a second important effort" that is, "bring[ing] to the fore questions of the ethics of representation and action that accompany compassion" (p. 11). This work requires that we, as educators, support students to be explicit about the narratives—about people, about places, about social issues, about themselves—they are constructing within engaged learning contexts. We must be explicit with ourselves about our own narratives; otherwise, we do a disservice to students and to ourselves when we fail to situate these experiences within larger contexts, especially ones that are steeped within white supremacist, patriarchal, capitalist underpinnings of inequity.

Thus, it is important for us to ask: Who and what do students, as social actors, represent in these narratives? Do they become

- innocent bystanders?
- obligatory student participants?
- **engaged learners?**
- change agents?
- activists and advocates?
- revolutionaries?
- **. . . or all of these with Revolutionary Minds?**

Where, how, and why are these narratives and this work taking shape? How are engaged pedagogy and learning, even on a local level, connected to (and not severed from) larger political issues that can have devastating consequences on a possible future guided by equity and justice?

Social ills become easier to dismiss when people unfortunately blame those who are suffering with being the root cause of their suffering. Utterances that begin, *"if they only tried harder, worked more, were politer"* and end with a complete release from suffering, roll off the tongue with racist framings deeply situated in the myth of meritocracy. For some, it is much harder to situate problems in their abstract realities, to anchor poverty in economic policies, part-time work, surging health insurance premiums and deductibles, and the influences of ableism within a capitalist framework that sees bodies as expendable commodities. Wrapping one's mind around a problem that is temporally and spatially removed from its causes and cleansed of the ideological forces is, in effect, keeping it intact. Protecting students from self-location in societal ills might appear to be neutral, but such moves actually coalesce around and reinforce ideologies such as ableism, racism, and sexism.

Boler (1999) is aware that there is a growing disdain for emotion in classrooms, yet when a pedagogical approach such as engaged pedagogies places it front and center, an educator can either spend energy trying to maneuver around it, to the detriment of students' learning, or spend energy integrating this important dimension of social transformation into learning opportunities. Mirra (2018) emphasized a similar orientation in her work by highlighting literacy:

> The idea that constructs like race and class will cease to structure the experiences and opportunities of individuals and communities if we simply ignore them and focus on our common humanity is not only misguided, but dangerous, for it both allows the stratification to continue *and* [emphasis added] attempts to silence the dialogue that is the first step in doing something about it. (p. 13)

Mirra proposes critical civic empathy, an orientation toward humanization where "teachers and students must engage together in reflection and action aimed at breaking down structures of oppression that ensnare us all" (p. 10).

In addition, Boler (1999) reminds us that "we must reevaluate what counts as knowledge for our students and whether or not emotional sensitivity and affective education represent crucial forms of epistemological awareness requisite to a transforming society" (p. 148). To ignore emotion is to ignore strongholds of oppressive ideologies. Boler criticizes classrooms, particularly those engaged in working toward equity that fail to facilitate students' awareness of their emotional responses, given that alienation, fear, anger, and despair lie at the root of domination.

It is helpful to visualize students and teachers along a continuum of empathy. Granted, some may not land on the continuum, but many do. Assuming that some students land on this continuum when they encounter other people through problem-posing education, engaged work, or social justice organizing, it is useful to understand the poles. On one end there might be a clustering of individuals experiencing passive empathy (Boler, 1999), disengagement (Ellsworth, 2004), naïve consciousness (Rosenberger, 2000), and consumption of the Other (Boler, 1999). At the other end might be critically conscious empathy (Rosenberger, 2000), critical civic empathy (Mirra, 2018), radical empathy (Cargle, 2020), and labor of response (Ellsworth, 2004).

It is important to know where students are situated on the continuum and how they might describe themselves so that educators can help facilitate self-reflection. If inclined toward passivity, then action and thought might be confined to graded assignments and days in the community garden. Such an orientation might lead educators to co-identify different sets of readings, codesign different sets of prompts, and co-facilitate different kinds of conversations, than say, the readings, prompts, and discussions facilitated with a group of students inclined toward organizing, self-reflection, and action. Like most classroom learning, differentiation that is firmly and fully steeped in equity and justice is necessary.

RESTORATION

At Liberty High, the obvious fracture between the purpose of the community garden and its original design existed in plain sight for several years, as do many of the contradictions between our commitments and our actions, as well as partially realized democratic visions that insist on equity and inclusion. By laying the groundwork for engaged learning, which began with Ms. Washington answering the phone call from a community partner across the street from the school, Ms. Washington refined her pedagogical approach. She invited students into critical noticing and organizing around shared commitments. She encouraged them to participate in restorative work within community spaces. They collaborated to mend tears between academic and community literacies, schools and families, and among thoughts, feelings, and actions.

The learning opportunities we have described in this chapter are not intended to be an exhaustive list of the engaged pedagogies that students should be afforded. Instead, they are intended to be illustrative of the generative nature of learning at the hyphen (e.g., Fine, 2018; Jones & Jenkins, 2008; Kinloch, 2009, 2010) and the improvisational collaboration it can inspire for teachers, researchers, community partners, students, and families.

Paula, the pastor mentioned at the beginning of this chapter, remembered how the vandalism on church walls and church grounds had

With a Revolutionary Mind: Literacies, Communities, and Engaged Pedagogies

Community Garden **by Grace D. Player**

ceased since the beginning of the project. She described, "Spray painted pentagram on the side of the church kind of stuff. Like ridiculous kind of stuff." Paula continued, "We haven't had one problem in five years. Not one. You can't tell me that's a coincidence. It's the same time frame!"

Ms. Washington shared that Mr. Alston, the principal at Liberty High, "heard Pastor Franks [Paula's colleague] say, the theft at the church has gone down to nothing since we've been doing [the projects]."

We believe that Paula's sentiments and Mr. Alston's reflections regarding decreased vandalism and theft point to a larger concern embedded within some school-community relations—that is, how one sees, perceives, and interacts with *unknown* others. For instance, Paula may have initially perceived students at Liberty, and students at Liberty may have initially perceived Paula and members of the church, through a narrow (maybe racist and classist) gaze. In the absence of engaged pedagogies and engaged projects, such ways of seeing were not challenged, questioned, or critiqued. With engaged pedagogies and engaged projects, conversations about self, others, and the world emerged, and assumptions about raced bodies were interrogated through empathy.

Additionally, while members of the Team were skeptical about whether or not their efforts had a "yeasty" effect on their peers and school culture around ableism, these particular accounts suggest that such an effect was possible. They also suggest that engaged pedagogies and school-community collaborations involving students, teachers, and community partners, all of whom are learners, can result in revolutionary understandings of self in relation to others and the world—*with a revolutionary mind!*

With these things in mind, we end this chapter with a few questions for you to consider:

- How do you invite students to enter into engagements with you, with each another, and with community partners?
- **What are their beliefs, values, and attitudes about community, engagement, and learning?**
- What are the concrete limit situations that students seek to address in their learning, and how might stories from their lives intersect with these situations?
- What is the range of feelings present in this work?
- How can you invite students to see these feelings as sites of inquiry and understanding, as well as rooted in engaged pedagogies?

"Change, Changes, Changing": Our Found Poem #4

Offered by Valerie, Emily, Tamara, and Grace

Waiting for what?
For you
For me
For us
To work in community
"Because I am you"
And you are me
And together
We will change the world.
The world.

Change.
Changes.
Changing.

Let's go!

CHAPTER 4

"Because I Am You"
Engaged Pedagogies and Critical Youth Organizing Literacies

> Thank you for those who helped us put this in place because without the help of the community, this wouldn't be possible. I see you. I hear you because I am you! ("Local teens")

On June 4, 2020, a group of six teenage girls referred to as *Teens for Equality*—Jade Fuller, Nya Collins, Zee Thomas, Kennedy Green, Emma Rose Smith, and Mikayla Smith—co-organized and co-led a Black Lives Matter protest against white supremacy in Nashville, Tennessee. It attracted more than 10,000 participants (Alund et al., 2020; Laparra, 2020). The march opened with 15-year-old Zee Thomas exclaiming, "As teens, we are desensitized to death because we see videos of black people being killed in broad daylight circulating on social media platforms. . . . As teens, we feel like we cannot make a difference in this world, but we must" (Renkl, 2020).

Two days later, on June 6, 2020, three teenage girls—Ariana Belyue, Mary Vucaj, and Angel Santana—co-organized and co-led a march for justice that included approximately 5,000 people on a 2-mile stretch in Sterling Heights, Michigan (Elrick & Robinson, 2020). During the march, 16-year-old Ariana Belyue passionately stated, "When you see people in your community standing with you for something you believe like this, it feels good. . . . America was built off a lot of racism that people really don't understand."

These two protests each resulted from exchanges that occurred in group chats, on Twitter posts, or via cell phones by young girls who sought ways to rally support for Black lives mattering within systems that continue to harm, abuse, and kill Black people. For us, these protests, among so many others happening across the globe, serve as public reminders of the violence perpetuated against Black people in this country, to include, as the founders of the Black Lives Matter movement describe, "Black queer and trans folks, disabled folks, undocumented folks, folks with records, women, and all Black lives along the gender spectrum" (https://blacklivesmatter.com/about/). Additionally, these protests magnify the voices of young people who are just as horrified as we are by the violent interactions that one too many Black persons have had and continue to have with law enforcement, especially in this country. Lest we forget that on March 13, 2020, 24-year-old Breonna Taylor was shot and killed when Louisville, Kentucky, police officers erroneously entered her home searching for a suspect in a drug case. Two months later, on May 25, 2020, 46-year-old George Floyd, a Black man handcuffed while facedown on the ground, was murdered on camera by Minneapolis, Minnesota, police officers. The murder of Ms. Taylor and Mr. Floyd are but two of many other examples of why we must intervene by way of teaching, protesting, marching, resisting, and changing racist policies in systems of educational inequities, social inequalities, and deadly violence against Black people.

We are deeply impacted by the commitments of these young people—from Jade Fuller, Nya Collins, Zee Thomas, Kennedy Green, Emma Rose Smith, and Mikayla Smith in Nashville, to Ariana Belyue, Mary Vucaj, and Angel Santana in Sterling Heights—to organize, lead, and protest against violence and in support of productive democratic change for freedom.

As *New York Times* contributing opinion writer Margaret Renkl (2020) asserts:

> These young people are passionate about their causes and unwavering in their commitment to change. The world they have inherited is deeply troubled and desperately flawed, and they see with clear eyes both the errors of earlier generations and the hope of their own. Their power lies in the undeniable moral authority of youth: They did not cause the mess they have inherited, but they are rolling up their sleeves to clean it up.

Indeed, their activism is marked by their commitment, passion, and desire for change. It provides educators and researchers, especially those of us whose work is situated within literacy studies, literacy teacher education, and ELA instruction, with opportunities to learn with and from young people about ways to

BLM by Grace D. Player

ADVOCATE.
Collaborate with others to address urgent public concerns and problems.
Organize and strategize for transformative, productive short- and long-term change.
AGITATE.
Galvanize people (including ourselves) to participate in community-based and systems-level work.
Imagine and create better, different, justice-directed futures.
Cultivate critical youth organizing literacies.
ACTIVATE.

And, yet we wonder: Did these young people learn these strategies and organizing literacies inside classrooms and schools? Did they learn about the role of engaged pedagogies within their extended school and extracurricular learning experiences?

Maybe they did. Maybe they did not.

Nevertheless, these young people can teach us quite a bit about the praxis of what Butler (2017) refers to as "critical youth organizing literacies" (CYOL). In her work with BLTL World Humanities educators and high school students at Justice High School, Butler conceptualizes CYOL as "acts of critiquing texts and cocreating new meanings around texts in mobilizing efforts" (p. 84). Zee Thomas from the Black Lives Matter Nashville protest, for instance, both activates and embodies CYOL in her public declaration that "As teens, we feel like we can't make a difference in this world, but we can and we must. Once again, we like to thank you all for joining us and giving us the opportunity to show the world that we are the newest generation and that we will make change" ("Local teens," 2020).

Standing before the gathered crowd at Bicentennial Capitol Mall State Park, Zee acknowledges that there are pervasive narratives *about* teenagers, some that are negatively internalized *by* teenagers as well, that unfairly portray them as apathetic, disengaged, and too young to incite social change. In the face of such narratives, Zee and her co-organizers, Jade, Nya, Kennedy, Emma Rose, and Mikayla, enacted new meanings of youth activism, youth political identities, and youth organizing (see Baldridge, 2019). Their collective declarations for justice for Black lives remind us, in the words of Tuck and Yang (2013), that "people who are under age 18 (the legal age ascribed to adulthood in the Unites States, although some rights are withheld until age 21) are whole thinking, feeling, and being people" (p. 178). In the streets and within communities, in schools and on social media, we have many examples of "youth as contemporary change agents" who are raising questions about "sustainable spaces to engage in social justice work" (Butler, 2017, p. 84). Unfortunately, some educators might miss opportunities to be inspired by young people to rethink *how*, *what*, and *why* we teach, and how our teaching should include reconfigured space-time relations for equity and engaged learning (see Chapter 5). Some educators might also miss opportunities to invite students to analyze forms of oppression within readings and to interrogate injustices within local and global contexts, to also include, honestly, within the contexts of their very own schools.

Simply acknowledging that there is a rift between classrooms and the streets is the equivalent of placing a construction cone in a 5-foot crater or a "Rough Road" sign on a street lined with debris and potholes. We must move beyond acknowledgement and into productive action. In this chapter, we engage in this movement by considering how classrooms can learn from the streets, or communities, about becoming places and spaces in which students can more fully articulate their visions for themselves and be supported to mobilize their energies as they seek freedom in the present moment and into multiple futures. We emphasize that working *with* and learning *from* young people requires that we engage in a radical reimagination of what teaching and learning are, which can happen through critical listening, open dialogue, and, as we described in the previous chapter, catalytic empathy. Indeed, working *with* and learning *from*, which require us to trust, believe in, care about, and love young people, point to engaged pedagogies and cross-generational modes of liberation. When we engage in this work within schools, classrooms can become interactive spaces where imagination, listening, and dialogue pave the way for students to dream about and enact desires for equity and justice. Students and teachers can cultivate youth organizing literacies, and engaged pedagogies can serve as significant springboards for this necessary work.

TIME TRAVEL

As you read this chapter, you may feel as if we are engaging in time travel. We shift between current and past learning experiences to consider the kinds of engagements and engaged pedagogies that are required to cultivate critical youth organizing literacies. We begin with a discussion of how imagination allows us to hear, think, and be present with young people, and how listening deeply impacts our classroom culture, climate, and exchanges. We intentionally and lovingly listen to 9th-graders imagine and describe their conceptions of social justice in a World Humanities classroom with BLTL educators. Our listening is important for the following reasons:

- **It allows us to attend to, embrace, and learn lessons shared with us from 9th-graders.**
- It encourages us to determine ways to not only use engaged pedagogies in our own teaching but also to enact these pedagogies and lessons from young people in teacher preparation programs.
- It also motivates us to remain committed to cultivating critical youth organizing literacies in classrooms and communities by listening to and seeing youth **in the present moment and in our thinking toward futurity.**

- It allows us to witness how the sharing of stories makes space for **truth-telling** and, simultaneously, impacts how we reimagine, refigure, and rebuild schools.

From our discussion, we then turn attention to some creative young people in a World Humanities course at Justice High School. We are drawn to their efforts to rearticulate the realities of environmental racism and human sex trafficking through popular music. We are inspired by their use of sophisticated visual rhetorics to critique behaviors and beliefs connected to domestic violence, LGBTQIA discrimination, and factory farms. Alongside their teachers, approximately 50 students disintegrated the walls between school and community to explore these injustices at a local level. In this chapter, we turn our attention to six of those students who invested in learning about and advocating against environmental racism, cyberbullying, and gentrification. Collectively, they demonstrate what is possible when given the space and time to think about the past and present and to imagine more equitable and just futures.

IMAGINATION AND THE IMPOSSIBLE: YOUTH FUTURES

In "Black Girl Ordinary: Flesh, Carcerality, and the Refusal of Ethnography," Savannah Shange (2019) calls our attention to imagination as a central driving force in abolition work. Particularly within prisons, abolition work requires individuals and institutions to divest from exploitative labor and corporeal treatment that mark incarcerated bodies as fungible. It also requires that we see and commit to other versions of people. In other words, we must invest in reconciliation, rehabilitation, and other ways of undoing and unlearning toxic ideologies that we may not have language for—yet. It is crucial that social justice practitioners as well as critical literacy teachers and researchers do similar work of divesting, but from limited conceptions of young people as immature, unteachable, unruly, and unconcerned. Consequently, we must also divest from ideas of "impossible futures" (p. 12), which, for Shange, means divesting from the inability to see young people beyond the present moment. That is, we must resist the tendency to make negative assumptions about young people's perceived behaviors in schools as indicators of who they will be and become in their future lives.

Shange (2019) turns our attention to Kate, a white female science teacher from the U.S. Midwest who "was part of the right-wing (read: liberal) flank of three of four Robeson [Academy] staff members who were invested in racial equity but saw individual agency as a key path to social change" (p. 10). She asks Kate to share why she thinks Tarika, a 16-year-old Black girl, was expelled from school. After characterizing Tarika as a quick-to-anger, easily agitated teenager, Kate continues: "It's hard for me to imagine her in the world. . . . It's hard for me to imagine her, I don't know, interacting with outsiders. And I think that's really scary" (p. 13). We (Valerie, Emily, Tamara, and Grace) are hyper-troubled by Kate's racist reading of Tarika for many reasons, in particular, because Tarika was **NEVER** a student in any of Kate's classes. According to Shange, "All of [Kate's] encounters with her were disciplinary, and mostly happened in the hallways" (p. 10). In addition, because Kate makes assumptions about Tarika's present and future—she believes "Tarika's story" has already been written, **AND** Kate "still preemptively indicts her for its lack of a happy ending: her vision of Black girlhood is evacuated of agency, dripping with blame" (p. 13).

We are also drawn to Shange's analysis that Tarika thus becomes "unthinkable"—unable to be conceptualized beyond this moment, unable to grow into an adult, and unable to be positioned beyond the geographies of the school and the city.

When we begin to divest from "educational survival complex" (Love, 2019), we begin to unlink classrooms from the carceral geographies and ideologies that police young bodies and relegate them to this contemporary moment. We open up space to think in the present and the future. In doing so, futurity is not something for which we must prepare young people. Instead, it becomes a multifaceted possibility where we think and work together toward futures. We *see* young people with futures, and we partner with young people to make space available for them to not only imagine but also to design, create, and enact those futures. It is here that we are reminded of Tiffany Nyachae's (2019) call to educators to "Listen to what young people tell you about how they perceive their world, realities, and academic experiences" (p. 109).

As literacy teachers and teacher educators, the uptake of engaged pedagogies can only be mobilized by those who have the desire to hear, conceptualize, and genuinely acknowledge how young people are already interacting within and understanding the world. When we truly tune into what young people are dreaming of, developing, and

We Deserve by Grace D. Player

enacting, then we can intentionally move closer to what is possible. We take this commitment to *what is possible* into our work with BLTL educators and students.

And we enter into Justice High School.

ESTABLISHING CONTEXT: JUSTICE HIGH SCHOOL AND BLTL

Focused on collaborative learning, Justice High School opened in the late 1980s. It is located on a 50-acre campus that is only minutes away from the Corridor, a historically African American community that, during the time of our Bringing Learning to Life (BLTL) initiative, was undergoing urban renewal. Like its neighboring community, Justice High has continuously faced expansion, development, and change, given its location within this midsize midwestern city. During the time of our BLTL work, Justice High had a student population of 604, which was categorized as 77.9% Black, 1.7% Hispanic, 18.1% white, and 2.3% "other" (the district referenced other as Asian American, American Indian, multiracial and multiethnic, and immigrant students). As a lottery school, students at Justice High lived in different neighborhoods within the district. However, the school was classified as a "high poverty school," a classification that did not tell accurate stories about the school, its teachers, its students, and its commitment to engaged pedagogies. It was also a classification that required us to turn to the World Humanities class, among other classes, to get a more complex picture of the kinds of engagements that occurred within the school, especially as we thought deeply about critical youth organizing literacies, equity, and justice.

Out of approximately 200 students enrolled in 9th grade at the school, 52 were in the World Humanities course, co-taught by four teachers: Ms. Prince, a white woman who was an intervention specialist and a BLTL educator; Mr. Merry, a white man who taught social studies and a BLTL educator; Mrs. Penn, an African American woman who taught ELA; and Mr. Sapien, a white man who served as a special education teacher. Because of his active involvement in BLTL, Mr. Merry would regularly talk about his students, the topics they researched, and the multiple literacies that flourished within the school and community. The World Humanities classroom was steeped in a social justice curriculum and was always filled with discussions about students' research and advocacy efforts against domestic violence, human sex trafficking, animal abuse, bullying, racial injustices, environmental damage, and gentrification, among other topics.

Although the World Humanities course focused on world history from 1750 to the present, it was cross-disciplinary, as students were expected to meet state Academic Content Standards for Social Studies **and** English Language Arts. In an effort to creatively "demonstrate command of social studies and English skills and methods, including research" (according to the course description), students were supported to propose, develop, design, and present Social Justice Capstone projects throughout the academic year (see below for a description of some of the projects). Their projects were not only brilliantly designed, conceptualized, and shared with others at the school and in the community, but they were also representative of their learning alongside teachers in a course that centered, every single day, on engaged pedagogies.

REFLECTIONS FROM THE WAKE: BLTL AND THE WORLD HUMANITIES CLASS

> "Social justice is/means to me a problem that should be made known to people. A problem that should be solved through teamwork and participation by people who share the same feelings toward the situation, and to encourage others to join." Ysende, 9th-grade student

The preceding quote is from Ysende, a Black girl who was one of the 52 9th-grade students enrolled in the World Humanities class. Students and teachers had just finished reading, discussing, and debating Marjane Satrapi's (2003) *The Complete Persepolis* and examining the outcomes of the Cold War. To build on their discussions of the texts, students separated into groups where they received index cards with the following questions: "What do you think 'social justice' means? What do you think of when you see or hear the term 'social justice'?" The opening quote to this section was what Ysende carefully penned on her card.

In groups of four or five students, each team developed a capstone project that tackled a different social justice issue (Butler et al., 2020). It is not lost on us that Ysende, the student cited previously, was offering this reflection *while* thinking with team members about environmental racism. She was keenly aware that addressing injustices and inequities requires collective action and a collective mind, or as she explained, "participation by people who share the same feelings toward the situation." Ysende was a member of a team that was passionate about issues of clean air, limited recycling options, and the presence of hazardous waste sites near predominately Black and Brown working-class communities in the city.

Throughout the class sessions, teams of students *moved toward* social justice by working on 10 different issues, such as cyberbullying, human sex trafficking, neighborhood pride, and LGBTQIA rights. The project's multi-issue approach offered a model of what engaged, justice-oriented work could look like in practice. Too often, we discuss and teach about social justice as unidirectional and linear—if we can tackle and solve issue #1 first, then we can move to issue #2. However, reflections from the World Humanities class demonstrate that it is unnecessary to work on one issue at a time. In fact, it is more than possible and, we believe, even necessary, to take an intersectional approach to working on related issues that move students and teachers toward more equitable, accessible, interconnected, and responsible worlds.

Some of Ysende's classmates also echoed her sentiments about social justice. Other students penned the following responses on their index cards:

- "Social justice is not something to be taken lightly. It is an issue that people either don't know about or don't care to do anything about it."
- "Bringing attention to an important issue."
- "Social justice means a problem that we have and that needs to be fixed."

Social justice, for Ysende and her peers, is an urgent issue that requires collective attention and action. Therefore, as we consider the rich possibilities of engaged pedagogies, we became captivated by the work occurring with students and teachers in the World Humanities classroom at Justice High. We were inspired to increase our focus on engaged pedagogies after hearing students' reflections about what they believe advocacy and activism require and what they see as essential to their learning with one another.

Days before students in the World Humanities class received index cards asking for their understandings of social justice, they discussed acts of genocide—on the Day of Silence. All 52 students shuffled, ran, and shuttled into their seats in the large, open classroom space, with their mouths covered—some donning purple tape, some opting for rainbow tape, and one wearing tape showing a camouflage-colored zipper. The class gradually quieted as Mr. Merry reviewed the homework assignment, "Analyzing Acts of Genocide." Students helped to complete the matrix projected on the board by recording their responses on notebook paper or on the personal dry-erase boards. Some used the time to take sneak peeks at their phones or scribble notes on their classmates' papers.

As Mr. Merry transitioned from 1992 Bosnia to the 1994 Rwandan Genocide, a student not wearing tape over her mouth broke the silence with the question, "How did the government get normal people to murder their neighbors?" One of the special education team teachers, Mr. Sapien, offered a brief reminder of the Stanley Milgrim experiment as a way to invite students to consider the jarring question on the floor.

>Silence and little to no movement followed.

Mr. Merry encouraged students to think more locally (as in the present and in a closer context), when he asked, "Well, why don't people speak up against . . . bullying?"

A dry-erase board pierced the air with "give up right to authority" written in green marker. A worn and stuffed notebook air waved back and forth with a question, "Could it be that they don't have to take the blame?"

Mr. Sapien interjected with, "A term in social psychology—what is it called?" Two students attempted to answer with "Group think" and "Bystanders" written on pages of their notebooks, covered with other doodles and scribbles. Mr. Sapien answered his own question, ". . . called diffusion of responsibility."

Mr. Merry continued to urge students to think locally: "What can we do? Today is a good time to talk about it." Little did we know, hours after the school bell rang to signal the end of the day, the Day of Silence would extend to the lives lost in the streets of Massachusetts as two bombs detonated at the Boston Marathon. Another moment, less than 2 months removed from the murder of Trayvon Benjamin Martin, made us ask questions about humanity and our relationships to one another as human beings.

When asked to complete the index card with a definition of social justice, six days after the Day of Silence, Jackson, a white boy in the class, wrote: "Social justice is treating all sentient beings with respect."

As a member of the group studying and advocating for an end to cyberbullying, Jackson shared that all human beings who can feel and perceive things deserve respect. His group members were drawn to the unfortunate uptick in young people committing suicide after being harassed, teased, and mocked on social media for being "different" from their peers. What was compelling here is that this definition came from Jackson, a student with an identified learning disability who worked closely with the team's special education teachers. Because Jackson sat in the last row of shared desks in the classroom, he may have missed the eye-rolling and looks some of his classmates exchanged with one another each time he raised his hand. However, he definitely sensed their aggravation or disdain when a teacher signaled for his answer.

When he wrote "treating all sentient beings with respect" on his index card, he may have recalled the snickering, teeth sucking, or exacerbated sighs that he often had to speak over as he maintained eye contact with his teachers who assured him that they were listening and that they cared. Their daily uptake of engaged pedagogies and their discourse of care comforted Jackson.

Though 8 years and 400 miles removed from Nya in Nashville, Tennessee, Jackson and Ysende at Justice High School, as well as countless other young people across the globe, remind us that injustices arise from the unwillingness to recognize one another as "levelly human" (Combahee River Collective, 1971), that is, as a person fully worthy of respect. In outlining the premise of Black Feminism and the beliefs of the Combahee River Collective (CRC), members of the CRC emphasized that they were not interested in respectability politics, which demanded superiority ("queendom" and "pedestals"), or in perpetuating the current state of inferiority. Instead, they—Black lesbians, women who loved women, other Women of Color—demanded the same treatment, legal protection, and freedoms as men, as white people, and as people who identified as heterosexuals. They wanted, for instance, to live in a world where they could embrace who they loved without persecution, where they would receive the same pay as a man and/or a white woman who did the same job, and where they could thrive in a world by having the right to choose whether or not they would bear children. Members of the CRC provide us, as well as students in the World Humanities class, with a keen awareness of how marking people as *different* and as *less than human* has lethal consequences.

ENGAGING ACTIVIST RHETORICS: CYBERBULLYING AND NEIGHBORHOOD PRIDE

In the months leading up to the social justice projects, at least 10 teenagers in the United States and Canada committed suicide in response to the overwhelming weight of being taunted, harassed, and blackmailed inside schools and through social media. Unfortunately, some of them were also sexually assaulted, and their assailants later posted videos and photos of said violence on the Internet. On the heels of the state's Anti-Harassment, Anti-Intimidation, and Anti-Bullying substitute house bill, three students at Justice High School decided that they wanted to do something to counter this trend of traumatizing and tormenting peers to their deaths.

Using Chris Brown's 2011 song, "Beautiful People" for their Revolutionary Music Project, students called attention to self-love and communal acceptance. After playing the song for the class, one of the group members emphasized that the "artist is trying to encourage" those who are "always being discouraged." Another group member added, "Remember 'you're beautiful'" and "what's on the outside doesn't matter as much as what's on the inside." While the latter part of the comment teeters on the edge of color-blind rhetoric (the falsity of "I don't see race"), here it serves an invitation for us to consider the possibilities and affordances of differences. Instead of using differences to divide and isolate people, students in the World Humanities class insisted on using it as Black feminists (Carruthers, 2018; Combahee River Collective, 1971; Jordan, 2002; Lorde, 1984; Smith, 1989) have advocated that we should: as a catalyst to organize and dismantle systems of oppression and inequality.

At the end of the academic year, this group's final project emphasized the prevalence and fatal outcomes of cyberbullying. Their art installation—a boxing glove punching through an old computer screen with notes scattered across the keyboard—highlighted the destructive nature of what we post and share on the Internet. With regard to critical youth organizing literacies, their work engaged a sophisticated visual rhetoric that called us to examine our relation to the issue. At one level, we initially read the piece as only about the victims or survivors who were deeply impacted by the violent blow of bullying that came through the computer. In sitting with the image, students asked us to consider what other circumstances might place *us* on either side of the boxing glove. We were invited to reevaluate our roles as viewers and consumers of the virulent images and verbal harassment and to consider the following:

- Do we become perpetrators when we watch, share, and/or scroll by?
- Do we place ourselves on the receiving end by advocating for victims and survivors?
- How do we feel and why?
- **Who do we become?**

Another group of students invited us to reevaluate our relations and roles with one another through their work on neighborhood pride. As previously mentioned, Justice High is located in very close proximity to a historically Black community that finds itself in the crosshairs of urban renewal-revitalization-gentrification. The three Black girls who made up this group asked us to think about the changing neighborhood through multiple lenses:

> New residents.
> Longstanding residents.
> **Displaced residents.**
> Neighboring community members.
> Legislators.

Singer-songwriter-performer Janelle Monae emerged as an advocate in this group's fight for community, as her 2010 song, "Dear Mr. President," took center stage in their Revolutionary Music Capstone project. For them, Monae's music comes across as concerned about the well-being of marginalized communities. When Monae sings about paying her rent tomorrow and being low on fuel, we believe she is signaling her frustration with events that are happening in the world and her dismay at being forced to choose between having housing and having food. Both should be affordable and accessible to all human beings. Sydney, a Black girl in the class, reminded us that "people are getting evicted" from their homes in these neighborhoods. Then, Aliyah, another Black girl in the group, drew our attention to the lines from Monae's song that, for Aliyah, get her to consider the high underemployment and unemployment rates in certain communities. Aliyah wondered aloud about why some people do not have access to food or affordable quality housing in a wealthy country that is so steeped in debt to humankind—to the very people who need us the most. Additionally, Aliyah uses Monae's lyrics to consider the structures that continue to negatively impact the historically self-sufficient Black neighborhood that lays in the fallout of white flight and now in the wake of urban renewal.

The World Humanities class was in the wake of racial violence clashing with post-racial (which some misconstrue as meaning that we live in a world that is "post-racism" or no longer impacted by racism) rhetoric (Butler et al., 2020), and students were acutely aware of how "the past that is not past reappears, always, to rupture the present" (Sharpe, 2016, p. 9). Although Barack H. Obama was completing his first term as president of the United States when Monae released this song, the country continued (not) dealing with the complications of racism, classism, sexism, transphobia, and xenophobia.

The past was rupturing the present.

The country's first Black commander in chief was still fighting to prove that he belonged in and to this country as birthers sought to denounce his citizenship and question his Blackness. Earlier in the same year, the World Humanities class explored connections among warfare, migration, and interstate construction. Therefore, they were quite familiar with ruptures and with the interstates that converged near their school campus, including the multilane one that separates them from the historically Black neighborhood for which they were researching and advocating. Before concluding their presentation, Aliyah posed a question to all the members of the class: "Why aren't you helping the community?"

Her group emphasized that social justice is a multifaceted endeavor guided by a desire to see, treat, and engage with each other as humans and "sentient" beings. The following student reflection encapsulates the overall purposes of the social justice projects students cocreated:

> "Social justice is what is fair and right.
> The good of people no matter how they are.
> Love of people no matter what. It is the opposite of injustice."

Social justice work, we contend, must be grounded in love and guided by the belief that people and systems can change. Engaged pedagogies are rooted in those same notions of love. Thus, our teaching and learning must emphasize change for "the good of people" who also deserve to be seen and treated as human beings working toward dismantling injustice.

RUPTURED LANDSCAPES, ENGAGED LEARNING

This chapter closes where it began. When Nya declared, "I see you. I hear you because I am you," she reminds us that young people are deeply impacted by what is happening in the world—violence, oppression, systemic racism. If we are to move toward a more equitable place, then we have to name, face, and work at eradicating the many inequities that exist, knowing that there are people attached to each and every one of them.

> "I am you" is an invitation for introspection.
> **"I am you" calls us to examine our intentions and actions.**
> "I am you" demands that we act and care in ways that are transformative and not performative.

Incorporation of multiple kinds of texts—that are antiracist and steeped in equity and justice, and grounded in freedom and liberation—in the midst of social unrest can be as performative as a placing a Black square on an Instagram account, making a photo op at a protest, sporting a cute safety pin, or kneeling in Kente stoles.

> "I am you" demands that we consider Nya (and other youth) as our present selves.

In fact, "I am" signals how we choose to engage in current decisionmaking choices and actions *with* and *for* others, either equitably or inequitably. We can decide that carefully clustered texts and experiences can invite students and teachers to work together to tackle issues of inequity and injustice and disrupt xenophobic thinking. Or, we can decide, unfortunately, not to. And when we decide not to, then we bear witness to horrific events such as the insurrection at the U.S. Capitol that occurred on January 6, 2021.

In other words, our working alongside, thinking with, and learning from youth is central to engaged pedagogical practices. Engaged pedagogies is not about the optics of engagement that may come from taking young people out of the classroom or using teaching strategies in hopes that students will think we are cool (Kinloch, 2018). Instead,

I Am You **by Grace D. Player**

engaged pedagogies is about being attentive to and interacting with one another through the lenses of futurity. We teach in ways that reflect deeply rooted beliefs that students will do more than exist in a world that is closer to equitable, empathetic, and liberated than this one. In order for our classrooms to "pulsate with multiple conceptions of what it is to be human and alive" (Greene, 1995, p. 43), we have to listen to, dialogue with, and imagine alongside each other. And we have to do this work through equity and because of justice.

The World Humanities projects and student reflections demonstrate that classrooms are shifting landscapes of learning, deeply informed by dispositions within and outside of the four walls of a school building. When we teach with an understanding that we are all learners working to positively transform the world, then classrooms can become dynamic spaces that reject the rushing floodwaters of zero tolerance school policies, corporatized standardized tests, and anti–public education legislation that seek to displace inquiry and dialogue with rigidity.

Students teach us to use and create texts to tackle contemporary moments, to rethink our beliefs, and to generate questions that

"Because I Am You": Engaged Pedagogies and Critical Youth Organizing Literacies

interrogate the ebb and flow of social unrest. These moments carve out holes, trenches, and pathways in educational landscapes. It is at these sites of rupture and with the ever-changing landscapes of teaching, learning, and engaging where students and educators teach each other to think about and to move toward collective possibilities.

With these things in mind, we end this chapter with a few questions for you to consider:

- How are you working alongside students and other educators to **ADVOCATE** and **AGITATE** for change within your school and local community?
- What does this look like and involve?
- What texts are you using in your classrooms and do they invite students to imagine a **BETTER,** more **EQUITABLE** world in which they can be and become who they want to in the present moment and into the future?
- What types of social justice projects are students **CREATING** and **PRODUCING**?
- How do their/our justice projects get us closer to deeper understandings of engaged pedagogies?
- What does "because I am you" mean?
- What does it imply about engaged pedagogies and critical youth organizing literacies?
- How do we make sense of time-space configurations in this work?

"Being Radical": Our Found Poem #5

Offered by Valerie, Emily, Tamara, and Grace

Waiting for what?
Engaged pedagogies and
Justice work.
Justice . . .
Where is the:
Justice?
Time?
Space?
For engaged pedagogies
and
Radical imagination
and
Radical Imagining
and
Radical love.

Being radical.

CHAPTER 5

Where Is the Justice?
Reconfiguring Time and Space for Engaged Pedagogies

Scenes

Act I

Scene I: Upheaval and Moments of Clarity

Act II

Scene I: Learningscapes
Scene II: Time
Scene III: Space

Act III

Scene I: Expanded Learningscapes and Networks of Practice

Cast

Elementary School Teacher	Ms. Streeter
Middle School ELA Teacher	Ms. Reed
High School ELA Teacher	Ms. Washington
High School ELA Teacher	Ms. Davis
Community Partner	Pastor Paula
Community Partner	Park Ranger Crystal
Community Partner	Ms. Jams
Community Partner	Mr. Ferguson
High School Student Travelers	Angela, Benjamin, Brendan, Jordan, Sarah, Tanya, and Kristopher

There can be no love without justice (hooks, 2018, p. 19).

Physical matters, matters of fact, matters of concern, matters of care, matters of justice, are not separable (Barad, 2013, p. 17).

UPHEAVAL AND MOMENTS OF CLARITY

In the previous chapter, we end with the question, "How do we make sense of time-space configurations in this work?" That is, how do we think differently about the rigidity of time and space as we take up the work of engaged pedagogies in classrooms and communities? In thinking differently, can we refigure the rigid boundaries of schools in ways that better attend to and center the many lives and realities within our communities and across the world?

>These questions take us first to the year 2005.
>**Hurricane Katrina. Category Five.**
>Alabama, Louisiana, and Mississippi.
>The levees. The flooding. The lost lives.

Following the devastating impact of Hurricane Katrina on the U.S. Gulf Coast, actor Danny Glover used his public platform to issue a statement about the persistence of racism and inequality and their adverse effect on human lives across the South and especially in New Orleans. Cutting to the heart of human suffering, Glover stated: "When the hurricane struck the Gulf, and the floodwaters rose and tore through New Orleans, plunging its remaining population into a carnival of misery, it did not turn the region into a Third World country, as it has been disparagingly implied in the media" (Taylor, 2020; see also Fothergill & Peek, 2008; Reich & Wadsworth, 2008). Instead, Glover insisted, "It revealed one. It revealed the disaster within the disaster. Grueling poverty rose to the surface like a bruise to our skin" (Taylor, 2020). Hunger, lack of quality and affordable health care for all, absence of shelter, and a weakening public infrastructure, including the levees, had been threatening people's lives long before the hurricane arrived. These realities were not unique to New Orleans and the Gulf Coast of August 2005.

For Dyson (2006), Hurricane Katrina revealed how "some of the poorest folk in the nation, people in the Delta, have been largely ignored, rendered invisible, officially forgotten" and, unfortunately, how "FEMA left them dangling precipitously on rooftops and in attics because of bureaucratic bumbling" (p. 4). He continues with the following:

> Homeland Security failed miserably in mobilizing resources to rescue Katrina survivors without food, water, or shelter. . . . But the government and society had been failing to pay attention to the poor since long before one of the worst natural disasters in the nation's history swallowed the poor and spit them back up. The world saw just how much we hadn't seen; it witnessed our negligence up close in frightfully full color. (pp. 4–5)

When the oceanic waters hit the Gulf Coast, they spilled over the storm walls, breached the levees, and overwhelmed the drainage canals designed to protect the residents and the properties along the shoreline. They flooded every surface, home, neighborhood, hospital, school, and business within reach, propelled by a strong hurricane force. The waters knew no boundaries.

And now to the year 2020.
A raging global pandemic.
More devastation and deaths.

More recently, the COVID-19 global pandemic has laid bare similar inequities and inequalities, particularly within the United States and with Black, Indigenous, Latinx, and other People of Color among the most impacted by the novel coronavirus. In other words, underlying racialized inequities perpetuated within and across social systems have led to a disparate number of People of Color being harmed and/or killed by the pandemic.[1]

In "A Meditation on the Mississippi Coast after Katrina," writer Natasha Tretheway (2008) speaks of her grandmother, who maps the stories of Hurricanes Camille (1969) and Katrina (2005) onto one another: "Between the two, there is the suggestion of both a narrative and a meta-narrative—the way she both remembers and forgets, the erasures, and how intricately intertwined memory and forgetting always are" (p. 7). We are also weathering and witnessing storms—anti-Black racism, classism, underemployment, an overextended health-care system, and more. Like Tretheway, we are curious about how "the storm(s) will be inscribed on the physical landscape as well as on the landscape of our cultural memory" (p. 7).

Essential Workers **by Grace D. Player**

Insofar as schools are concerned, the National Education Policy Center recently emphasized the disparate negative impact of COVID-19 on People of Color and students facing poverty, particularly those attending low-resourced schools where there would be insufficient personal protective equipment for all students, staff, and administrators. Teacher strikes punctuated the desperation many felt heading back into the classroom without the necessary supplies and supports to teach and learn in person, and some (but not all) were victorious, however temporarily, in drawing the line and standing at its edges. No masks? No school.

Both Hurricane Katrina and COVID-19 exposed dangerous, ongoing racist patterns to those people caught in the throes of struggle—patterns that connect (or disconnect) neighborhoods, towns, and cities from each other. They quickly exposed the root causes of the pain and violence, and the rooted systems of dehumanization and oppression entangled within the very foundation of many U.S. public schools. These supposed "natural" disasters also revealed unnatural outcomes (Buras, 2020), skewed data, and crises within crises, making clear why we cannot sit back and wait for the next natural disaster to register on a national or global agenda to insist that equity work is centered inside schools. The work must take center stage immediately. We have no other logical choice but to increase our efforts to analyze, unmake, revise, and rebuild our pedagogies alongside students, families, neighbors, citizen scientists, educators, and community leaders if we are to move toward more equitable futures. How this nation has responded to Hurricane Katrina, and even COVID-19, demonstrates that a scarcity mindset—falsehood that there is not enough money and resources for everyone—is similar to how some people have approached education as unfixable. Education is not unfixable. We have enough resources to remake and dramatically improve our educational landscape. However, we refuse to use those resources to save lives, end racism, and provide equitable learning opportunities for those who need us the most. We must do better!

As critical educators committed to equity and justice, we have tracked violence across geographies and pain across time. They are rampant. They surface in our daily exchanges with students as they talk about a parent who worked two, sometimes three, jobs in order to afford to send their child to college. Other students have talked about the young people they hold in their hearts, from their hometowns, who drive their own efforts to do well in schools as well as their intention to return home when they graduate. We have no doubt that this kind of pain and violence surfaces in conversations many teachers have with students. In the midst of this despair, we remain encouraged by the critical mass of educators within schools, communities, and other educational landscapes (or learningscapes, as we explain below) who are fully committed to equity work *with* students and families, and *in* and *with* communities. United by a shared concern for human dignity and life, countless educators encourage students to see further—beyond the walls of classrooms and schools, beyond streets and neighborhoods, beyond time, beyond gazes of negativity—into histories, desires, possibilities, and futures. As discussed in previous chapters, they partner with students to re-create, transform, and rebuild classrooms and communities into loving, life-affirming, and life-giving justice spaces for children, youth, families, and educators.

Thus, we use this chapter to consider the intentional moves BLTL educators made to reconfigure space and time in and beyond classrooms. These moves, which supported student learning and advocated for justice, represented educators' unwavering commitments to transcend space and time in order to imagine possible futures. We make sense of the learningscapes that emerged from this intentional work as relational places of learning where educators, students, and communities gathered—sometimes in concrete, visible ways, and other times in abstract, virtual, and symbolic ways—to move toward equity.

In this chapter, we emphasize how intentional and urgent this work must be: For Children. For Young Adults. For Families. For Communities. For Schools and Schooling. For Teachers and Education Leaders. For Activists and Advocates. **For Justice and Antiracist Teaching.** For All of Us.

HOW MIGHT THESE THINGS LOOK?

In our work, thinking expansively about how to support student learning to include time and space reconfigurations often felt a bit metaphysical. Unlike some of the resources educators use to support student learning (e.g., books, worksheets, pencils, and computers) that are easily counted, manipulated, and distributed among students, time and space as resources for learning are more abstract. Whereas the former things are requested of our students or acquired anew at the beginning of each school year, time and space are more obscure. They are often cast into the background, seemingly finite, fixed, and established: room numbers, bell schedules, seating assignments, and the names of educators printed onto students' schedules. Through the lens of engaged pedagogies, however, we can begin to see time and space as flexible and malleable or, at the very least, available resources to be mapped around students' visions for learning. Time and space—which are a part of our everyday experience, that is, "the water we swim in"—need to be at the front of educators' thinking. We can be creative in how we use time and space, given their fundamental roles in sense-making. And we know they are fundamental to sense-making, learning, human experiences, and, ultimately, to justice, because they were the very resources used in the strategies of civil rights' educators fighting for their communities and for their very own lives (see Chapter 3).

CIVIL RIGHTS' EDUCATORS

The work of educators and activists, such as Bernice Robinson and Septima Clark of the Citizenship Schools in South Carolina and Myles Horton of the Highlander Folk School in Tennessee, as well as young leaders such as Eddie James Carthan and Arelya Mitchell from the Freedom School movement in Mississippi (Hale, 2016), all centered on justice and issues of time and space. These rights' educators and activists were deeply invested in exposing the complexities of the issues they were studying, from systematic disenfranchisement of Black voters and exploitative labor practices in a capitalist system, to patterned, state-sanctioned removal of Black and Brown students from public schools. They engaged in community-organized forms of education that relied on a tridimensional understanding of issues across time: historicize it, understand how it operates in people's lives, and grasp the future or the "utopian performatives" (Muñoz, 2009) that remind us that "the present and presence . . . is not enough" (p. 100). They organized across geographies even as they imagined different geographies. They formed schools, unions, culture circles, and groups united in a shared struggle for freedom, justice, and liberation.[2]

These educators and activists remind us that we have a responsibility to envision and locate ourselves within justice-oriented futures, and to engage in humanizing forms of imagining and learning with others to get to those futures. They also remind us to **not** invest in schooling that polices and punishes bodies, and that manipulates time-space to meet standardizations while neglecting students' humanities. Thus, we are invested in learning that spans and crosses time and class periods; that centers collaborations with educators, students, and communities; and that is steeped in equity, justice, engagement, humanization, and care. We do not take the same approach to learning and engagement that has traditionally guided "schooling" over "learning," particularly in many parts of the U.S. educational system. Our focus on learningscapes is an intentional way to push for deeper analyses of how power becomes entangled in time-space relations and what we can do about it in the name of engaged pedagogies, justice, and equity.

To get there—that is, to these deeper analyses and enactments of justice—we must

- better account for space and time as learning resources,
- know that justice is necessary and must both be included in and guide our work,
- **understand freedom as a never-ending struggle that we must always pursue, and**
- realize that being free is not optional. It is necessary.

LEARNINGSCAPES: SETTING THE STAGE

We turn to learningscapes to better understand engaged pedagogies as embedded within space-time relations. Ms. Washington, the 9th-grade teacher who partnered with students to develop a wheelchair-accessible community garden and Disability Awareness Campaign, offers us an example. As she reflected on adopting an engaged approach to teaching and learning, she shared the following:

> I had an opportunity to form great relationships with my students, and I've given them the opportunity to make decisions about their classroom learning as a result of this project. To let them know that they matter inside of this classroom, I wanted them to participate in their own education. This project has also provided a huge platform for students to explore their ideas.

In foregrounding relationships with students, Ms. Washington first acknowledged that students are people in their own right—they are *not* adults in the making (Lesko, 2012). As referenced in Chapter 3, Ms. Washington was well loved by her students, some of whom referred to her as their second mom, and others called her their favorite teacher. She dismissed confident characterizations (Lesko, 2012) of adolescents as irrational beings driven by raging hormones or as people defined and contained by age. Instead, she took her students seriously and knew that they are fully capable of exploration, collaboration, decisionmaking, and action.

Her students saw this. They felt powerful in her presence and wanted to share their ideas with each other. In turn, Ms. Washington was always willing to rework her 9th-grade English curriculum to prioritize community-engaged projects, such as the garden and the Disability Awareness Campaign, because students were invested in them. One student, Kristopher, shared, "The best aspect of this is me working in the garden and experiencing how to communicate and work with my fellow classmates." Another student, Angela, reflected, "This has changed my attitude toward school a whole lot because at first I took coming to high school as a joke . . . and now I have the opportunity to communicate with other people and this is an opportunity to me." She went on to explain: "I can communicate with more students in our school and other people outside of school in the community."

Ms. Washington was not alone in how she engaged with students. There was also Ms. Davis, a BLTL educator and high school teacher at Katherine Johnson 9–12 Academy who believed students should have the right to think, explore, experiment, and engage with others inside and beyond the sanctioned time and space of school. This belief led Ms. Davis to embrace her high school students' request to cocreate a literature-art-beautification project that involved in-depth study of literary texts that they, themselves, would transform into live performances. A major goal of their project was to deepen connections among high school students (especially freshmen) and to use play and performance as strategies to engage with elementary-aged students who attended school and lived in their same neighborhood. Ms. Davis agreed to her students' project idea and sought ways to help them connect their classroom-based literary studies, discussions, and writings to the design and performance of a public play.

In one of her journal entries for our BLTL course, Ms. Davis wrote about wanting to support students to enhance their "higher level thinking that involves analyzing a text, evaluating effective ways to rewrite a text into a play-script, and creating a play to be performed for a children's and public audience." She continued, "the community will be served by this project" because it will allow "freshmen to have an outward focus for their community, bring a live art into [the school] to help with community revitalization, and promote connectivity to the pre-K–6 and 7–12 feeder pattern of the neighborhood schools that promotes the high school project-based learning program and promotes positive neighborhood pride." Like Ms. Washington and many of the other BLTL educators, Ms. Davis willingly reworked the curriculum to prioritize student needs and interests as well as community-engaged projects. Her commitment to student learning and engaged pedagogies was clear in how she actively collaborated with students, openly advocated for meaningful alignment between curricula and community engagement, and encouraged students to reject negative media portrayals of their very own communities. In these ways, she pushed herself and her students to reimagine constraining time-space dynamics within the classroom, which extended into the community.

These examples and many others from BLTL provide us with deeper understandings of connections among learning, space, and time within engaged pedagogies. Connecting and communicating with peers in the same classroom or with students in adjacent buildings was just the beginning of engaged pedagogies in action. Using the school day in service to learning rather than the other way around and encouraging students to gather as a way to see, feel, and interact *with* their communities further brought to life the promise of engaged pedagogies as opportunities to learn, relearn, unlearn, question, transform, and remake realities.

Among the many pedagogical considerations Ms. Davis, Ms. Washington, and other BLTL educators made to better integrate student ideas into the curricula, they were always thinking about time and space. They asked themselves: Would class time, the school day, and even the school year facilitate or constrain students' visions? Would there be enough time to do what students and teachers really wanted to do? Would classrooms afford the kind of movement and mobilities necessary for justice work? What would these things entail? How can time and space be experienced as learning resources?

In addition to these questions from BLTL educators, we (Emily, Grace, Tamara, and Valerie) have been asking ourselves related questions: Can educators be fully supported to foreground engaged pedagogies within institutions that do not actually value time-space *reconfigurations*? If so, then what would this look like? If so, then would this require a whole-system overhaul, and, if so, who would lead this effort? If not, then what are critical educators committed to equity, justice, and antiracist teaching with students to do within the confines of the existing systems? What about the school structure and administrative pressure for educators and students to "stay on task?" Are schools really the best place for this work to happen? What about Ms. Washington, Ms. Davis, their students, the communities, and their desires to teach and learn differently? To teach as justice? To learn for freedom?

WHAT ABOUT TIME?

For BLTL educators, reconfiguring time became critical to supporting student learning in engaged pedagogies. The reconfiguration often fell into one of three categories: (1) Needing more time, (2) Layering of time, and (3) Setting into motion new realities across time. In each of these cases, educators thought carefully about time and how to extend, layer, and use it to initiate new futures. Through the projects featured in this chapter, we showcase the value of time as a serious consideration for educators, students, and community partners. We also explore how they individually and collectively took up engaged pedagogies in practice.

More Time

Ms. Washington and her students met over the summer to prepare their application for a grant that was due in August. They had learned about the grant just after the current school year had ended, and it was due before the next school year began. Although the timing was not optimal, they agreed to meet during the summer to write the proposal for funds and in-kind labor from a hardware store that would support their community garden project. Witnessing the commitment of students and their willingness to collaborate during the summer, Ms. Washington reflected, "They have so much passion for this work that time doesn't seem to stop them. They see a need, they decide to meet it, and they did." Although students worked over the summer and not during the school year to secure grant funds, their "passion," to borrow Ms. Washington's word, must be considered within larger narratives about youth, time, and engagement. Many of the students worked in the summer and had to care for siblings, and they also determined how to reconfigure time to still work on the community garden project. They were all aware of the sustained time that the project needed, and they committed to it and to each other.

Undoubtedly, Ms. Washington's students prove to us that engaged pedagogies require time beyond traditional classroom time-space constrictions. One of their partners, Paula, who was working on a master of divinity (MDiv) at the time of their collaboration, also demonstrates how time is an important factor in engaged pedagogies. For her, one of the most valuable parts of the garden project was that it allowed sustained engagement with an idea:

> There's something to be said . . . especially with the garden, but in general, it takes *time*. Which is not something that the current high school curricula allow. I think there's value in letting students sit with an idea and work with that idea. It takes me a long time to sit, sometimes I have to sit with a problem, and stare at it and work through it in my head until I really know, you know? And I think service-learning allows young people to do that because it's actively staying with the same idea and the same focus. You're getting stuff done along the way. You know little goals here and there. But it has this continuous theme of you're staying with the same idea and working through that and processing that.

As Paula suggests, tackling an idea on any scale necessitates careful, methodical engagement over *time*. As a student herself, Paula was familiar with the importance of time as a condition for learning and as a dimension of the things learned. She was several years into her MDiv at the time of the collaboration, and her academic program in theology dealt not only in days, weeks, months, years, and decades—oft-used measurements of time in education—but centuries and millennia. Also embedded in her reflections were theories about how learning happens and a critique of the conditions in which some teachers find themselves: desires for deep, time-intensive exploration of ideas with students, even as time constraints push down on the work from every direction.

This theme, time constraints, also emerged for Ms. Davis. When asked about what she really hoped would result from the literature-art-beautification project with her high school students, she shared, "time to dig into other meanings of learning and about community." In her journal about the project, she explained that "the community defined here is a community often in transition and flux . . . but beaming with beacons of light and a desire to be viewed beyond those predominating issues and plight portrayed by the media." She described that it is a community that has received increased interest from city officials seeking to contribute to its revitalization. While she is excited to collaborate with students to think differently and positively about ways to *see* and *be* in the community, she does express agony with convincing other educators of the importance of rethinking time. This comes through in her pondering about whether students will stay after school to work on the project "because they just haven't had to before, and they've never been asked." Relatedly, she also worries that there will be "frustration from teachers for any needed time from the students that might be pulled from parts of their class" for this project.

As we reflect on our engagements with BLTL educators, we are aware of the combined eagerness and trepidation that many of them felt:

> But we need more time!
> How do I work around imposed time?
> How do we help administrators treat time in better, more useful ways?
> **What happens when the bell rings?**
> What do I do when students' learning gets interrupted and they don't want to stop?

What about when students are required to stop what they're doing and go to a class where they aren't being encouraged to learn with intention and care?
How do we get more time?
How can engaged pedagogies help us reimagine time and push against not having enough time?

Layering of Time

In addition to needing more time, engaged pedagogies take seriously the *layering of time* at work in all justice matters, particularly when it comes to the tridimensional nature we noted earlier of working historically in the present moment and keeping an eye toward futurity. Lemke (2000) reminds us that multiple timescales operate within classrooms simultaneously, some which are readily apparent, including the bell schedule, the academic calendar, and the sequence of a lesson. Others are more obscure because of how slowly they unfold around us (e.g., climate change, the public school system), within us (e.g., as our bodies age and our minds expand), and beneath us (e.g., as our school buildings inch toward repair). Within engaged pedagogies, these backdropped timescales sometimes spring to the fore as resources that contribute to our analyses and understandings of contexts.

When Paula, the community partner noted in the example of the community garden earlier, left the church, Crystal, a full-time park ranger at a local state park, took her place. Crystal's involvement provides an example of the layering of time. Two years into their project, students began working with Crystal. They studied eco-friendly ways to water the garden and to repurpose plastic barrels as rain barrels. Crystal explained the following to students:

> I'd like to build the beds out of the 55-gallon drums. Plastic drums. Cut in half. So you would have, the plastic will, you know, 55-gallon drums that are food safe, are designed to hold heavy wet things unlike wood that kind of deteriorates under that kind of pressure. So, you know, drill holes in the bottom of it, and I think it would be really cool, and [students] could design and decorate those beds, and that would be neat.

She drew students' attention out from the immediacy of the community garden into a larger timescale—that is, human-made climate change—to show them how their actions in the moment could have lasting effects into the future.

Similar to Crystal and Ms. Washington as well as Ms. Davis, Ms. Shawna Streeter (a veteran elementary school teacher who we briefly reference in Chapter 2) was concerned about the *layering of time* with engaged pedagogies as justice teaching and learning. Wanting to ensure that "her kiddos get outside to play and learn and experiment," she partnered with the Hallie Quinn Brown Settlement House to codesign the Living Healthy initiative. In one of her journal entries, Ms. Streeter explained that the local public health organization "has collected research statistics that identify [this community] as one of the most concentrated areas of risk (zip code) in the county." She goes on to write, "These statistics suggest a major health concern and focus of the United Way–supported health initiative that we need to take up immediately."

To take up this work, Ms. Streeter along with Ms. Jams, who was director of Senior Services at Hallie Quinn Brown Settlement House, and Mr. Ferguson, a community organizer and program coordinator there, explored ways to support residents' positive engagements with health and wellness. This exploration connected to the elementary school's curricular focus on STEM and guided their desires to "get students outside, walk, and learn outside of the school building" (Ms. Streeter) and to "get up, move, and foster intergenerational learning with kids and elders" (Ms. Jams). Valerie recalls meeting Ms. Streeter, Ms. Jams, and Mr. Ferguson at the settlement house and witnessing the Living Healthy initiative come to life. It was Ms. Jams who explained, "this will motivate our elders to keep active," and Ms. Streeter who echoed, "my kiddos are tickled they get to come here and make new learning buddies."

During this same meeting, Ms. Streeter excitedly shared her students' hopes ("to move around, talk to new people, to do healthy activities"), and Ms. Jams and Mr. Ferguson provided feedback from their surveying of elders at the Hallie Quinn Brown Settlement House about what they wanted to see happen (conversations with kids about what they want to become and how to move around safely). They agreed that the project question would be, "How can students and elders work to promote and influence each other to choose a healthy lifestyle?" This was layered with collective interests and desires to use available time differently—for learning as hands-on engagement. That is, they agreed to expand, extend, and remake existing timescales between the school and the settlement house. To do this, students walked with Ms. Streeter and an administrator from their school to the settlement house to participate in learning activities, conversations, and shared readings with elders. They participated in cross-generational exchanges during their in-person meetings. In the time between their meetings, elders wrote letters to the students and students drew pictures for the elders. Across six on-site visits to the settlement house, elders read aloud picture books about healthy lifestyles to the students. Students drew pictures depicting what they learned from the readings for the elders. They talked. They stretched. They exercised. They walked. They danced and sang, jumped up and down, and laughed together. They ate healthy foods together. They traveled to a healthy food store together and learned about buying and cooking fresh produce. They celebrated the end of their learning as engagement time together, and they hugged and cried. They became family.

Ms. Streeter and her community partners, Ms. Jams and Mr. Ferguson, worked in similar ways as Ms. Washington and her partners, Crystal and Paula. They all sought to create learning experiences that extended beyond the space of the classroom. These experiences were engaging and connected to the larger curricula; they were also grounded in understandings of time as an important dimension of learning. To Paula's credit, for example, it was through sitting with the garden as an idea that needed time to grow, and to Crystal's credit, it was using recycled materials to draw attention to climate as a matter of concern that was entangled in the need to keep the garden watered. For Ms. Jams and Mr. Ferguson, it was their commitment to providing quality elder services that led them into a brainstorming session with Ms. Streeter. Ultimately, this opened up the promise of engaged pedagogies as intergenerational learning experiences involving elementary students and elders who lived in the same community.

Setting New Futures Into Motion

The students in Ms. Washington's class credited the project with helping them to envision their futures. Brendan, Sarah, Tanya, and Kristopher collectively spoke to academic achievement, career aspirations, personal growth, and social action as all connected to their participation on the Design Team. Sarah specifically acknowledged her participation in the community garden and Disability Awareness Campaign as "show[ing] me what I want to be when I graduate."

Brendan explained that the projects "made me realize I needed to do something with my life," and Tanya reflected that she "came to school more and got good grades." Kristopher insisted it had moved him into productive and engaging action.

Ms. Washington shared the following sentiments about Brendan: "One of my students actually decided that he may want to actually enter the field of public speaking because he's had to do so much of it with the different presentations that we did." Brendan, who earned the nickname "The Planner" because of his ongoing participation with the projects from his freshman to senior year and because of how he shaped the work, often ended up center stage for public presentations. These experiences—being asked by his peers to represent the project to public audiences, being trusted to explain the project's commitments to engagement, being received with affirmation from peers and adults—facilitated a mapping out of a possible future for Brendan. This mapping out included his desire to become an orator who would share ideas for innovations with the world. In the diverse literacies and modalities of the project, public speaking was a stage where Brendan could shine, an academic exercise that facilitated a connection between his school life and his newfound aspirations.

Relatedly, at the end of the first year of the Healthy Living project, Ms. Streeter shared the following thoughts about the experience:

> My kiddos are so eager. When we went to the settlement house, there was uncertainty at first, but it's like we became familiar fast. Most of the kiddos were like, 'Oh, I know you, and I know you and you and you. I know all of you,' and that's because the elders mostly lived in their neighborhood. It was good to see that. . . . What was really good was seeing how my kiddos got into the project. If Ms. Johnson wasn't at the settlement house when we got there, they looked around for her and had stars in their eyes when she walked in. When it was time to dance, everyone was shy until Mr. Jackson started dancing in his chair, then the kiddos laughed so loud and went wild with excitement. Everyone started dancing, stretching, and exercising.

The various forms of participation that emerged from BLTL projects, such as exercising, intergenerational learning, reading, public speaking, activism, and advocacy set into motion futures that energized people toward specific goals, particular practices, and efficacious versions of themselves.

RECONFIGURING SPACE AS PLACE-MAKING

Engaged pedagogies require that we think beyond our immediate surroundings and facilitate with students' spatial extensions, spatial imaginations, and ultimately vast learningscapes beyond classroom and school walls. The first step in developing a more expansive view of space in engaged pedagogies requires that we ask students and ourselves the following question:

> In what directions do social justice matters require us to stand and act?
> **How can we fully narrate our visions for justice?**

We should also ask: How would students want teachers and peers to follow them there? Do students feel like teachers and peers are authentically looking inside classrooms, schools, local communities, and across the world to better understand space and time and their ongoing rootedness in injustices and inequities? In this looking, what do students and teachers hope would happen differently? **What are the justice paths forward and for what purposes?** Are there other more distant spaces and places that are being imagined, that we may have never been to, but can travel to, when dreaming of and wanting to experience equity and justice? These questions, we hope, unite us across geographies because of shared struggles, spaces, visions, and the learningscapes that extend out of necessity, for meaning-making, for equity, and because of justice.

We know that thinking beyond the walls of classrooms and schools is in tension with traditional, stereotypical views of embodied learning, which get perpetuated in film, by the media, and even in state and federal discourses. The stereotypical orientation of a student's body while *learning* is so ubiquitous that it is reified thousands of times in online image searches of "student learning"—bodies and eyes facing the front of the class, turned downward toward a text, or following the teacher around the room. A student whose head is turned away from the book is quickly redirected without question. The child who is out of her seat wandering and dreaming is reminded of the sometimes mundane writing task at hand.

A mind and body engaged in learning, though, looks very different depending on the pedagogical approaches of the teacher and the types of engagements and imaginings that are invited into learning spaces.

This leads us to insist that students must be free to move around classrooms as they come to

Connect and Create.
Think and Experiment.
Dialogue and Imagine.
Dream.
Access supplies.
And to simply move, breathe, and feel free.

Students should be able to freely move down the hallways to: The computer lab. The library. The cafeteria. To a welcoming teacher's class or a friend's safe embrace. The gymnasium. And they should also be supported to learn and thrive in virtual and/or hybrid environments. To wherever their justice imaginings and freedom dreamings take them, they should be supported.

Visions for Justice **by Grace D. Player**

Where Is the Justice? Reconfiguring Time and Space for Engaged Pedagogies

We are also familiar with the many learning opportunities that take us beyond classrooms, such as fieldtrips, internships, externships, visits to settlement houses, and learnings at grocery stores. How are they captured by the thousands of images produced by a simple image search of "student learning"? They are not!

Engaged pedagogies encourage us to think and move in dynamic, connected ways, but rather than being teacher-led, they encourage us to learn how to follow students' sites and sights. What if our pedagogical approaches call for movement *beyond* classrooms? Resourcing engagement through space means making available landscapes within and beyond classrooms that promote interconnectivity of matters of justice. Sometimes it means residing in the local and finding resonance in the global through technologies such as Google Earth and videoconferencing with teachers and students around the world. Whether it is physical travel or digital mobilities, the key is expanding the learningscapes methodically and in accordance with connections students are making in real time. We can do these things through and because of engaged pedagogies that are steeped in, committed to, and driven by investments in teaching and learning that are equitable, justice-filled, and antiracist.

Students in Ms. Reed's ELA class, discussed in Chapter 2, initiated another engaged project that took them around the world. Through virtual mapping tools, they traveled to Nike factories in other countries and on other continents. They discussed the ripple effect of a dollar spent on fast fashion in the United States on wages of workers around the world. On this topic, Ms. Reed explained to us that she "wasn't telling them not to buy Nike," but she did want them to see how spending a dollar locally was connected to labor practices globally. While some matters of justice appear to be contained by zip codes or a gerrymandered district, others are like groundwater, rippling below and across spaces, as in the example of watering the community garden.

Other movements beyond the classroom connected students with principals, community leaders, families, and district administrators. These served to build alliances for their engaged work. Angela, Benjamin, Brendan, Jordan, Sarah, Tanya, Kristopher, and many other students, for example, traveled locally and across the United States to attend and present at professional conferences; at meetings among principals, teachers, and board members; and within digital landscapes with district, union, and community leaders committed to making schools matter for students.

Reconfiguring space in these ways meant that students were tuning into their environments and relationships *wherever* they were located. In Ms. Washington's class, the community garden became a makerspace for learning where students dug, planted, pulled, shaped, scraped, walked, and sometimes ran. In Ms. Streeter's class, the settlement house became an important site for engaged learning *with* students and elders who read books, talked, danced, exercised, and made extended meanings *with* each other in relation to teaching and learning beyond traditional school spaces. They spent time at the Hallie Quinn Brown Settlement House, they visited a local health food/grocery store, and they walked the community that was already familiar to them in order to see it differently.

As we expand the spaces and places where we teach, learn, and engage with students, we further understand how the human body is integral to learning. We understand students' bodies (as we understand our own bodies) as making sense of, questioning, engaging with, and even at times, resisting environments. This is what it could mean to reconfigure space as place-making and as engaged forms of justice teaching and learning.

Ms. Washington, Ms. Davis, Ms. Streeter, Ms. Reed, and the many other BLTL educators were very accustomed to movement and expanded landscapes with students. They were accustomed to classrooms that were alive with voices, ideas, and movement. Their classroom spaces were so alive with voices that when students were working on their engaged projects, always present were the melodic sounds of voices—some voices were speaking into existence their hopes and desires for their projects, other voices were whispering aloud the strategies they contemplated putting into action concerning their collaborations, and still other voices were singing into the air big ideas and light bulb moments. These many different voices came from students interested in creating deeper connections between how they were feeling (in the moment) and how they were processing what they were designing (across various moments).

Their voices, sounds, and movements came so freely that in those very moments, they were not worried about being monitored and surveilled because they were not. According to Ms. Reed, "when I think about the work, I see how free my students are. They're excited to learn and talk about what they discovered. They're learning." For Ms. Reed and other BLTL educators, the focus was not on having students sit in desks in rows with eyes and bodies directed toward the blackboard and only toward the teacher. The focus was on engagement, discovery, and learning within spaces and across time that were conducive to what students needed and wanted to do, together. For Ms. Washington, students knew that they had freedom to explore and question. They also knew they were not going to be controlled and that their noise was central to their learning. The beauty of sound, movement, and wonderings—aloud and through whispers—were welcomed and embraced within and across these respective learning spaces.

EXPANDED LEARNINGSCAPES

Recasting the landscapes and timescales of learning in very explicit ways helped expand students' interests with learning and their development of critical understandings of how inequities spread across histories, lived conditions, and geographies. This recasting encouraged students to examine how inequities creep into and become violently entangled within futures. We want to be clear that by encouraging expanded learningscapes, we are **not** suggesting a colonizing state of mind. The language of expansion here is not about taking, claiming, or owning; it is **not** about aggressive, violent, uninvited, and manipulative actions. It is about alliances, connections, collaborations, and solidarity-building. It is about extending invitations and nurturing relationships *with* people wherever and whenever they are within, across, and beyond the confines of time-space dynamics and in relation to envisioning and enacting equity.

Reaching beyond their classrooms and school days, BLTL educators and students became connected to other learners within and beyond their schools, including professors, graduate students, district and union leaders, families of classmates, and other community leaders. They addressed various topics, including human sex trafficking, the lack of support for people with disabilities in an ableist society, healthy lifestyles, and the lack of transparency that accompanies acquiring philanthropic support for community-engaged work. Promoting student mobility across time and space not only expanded students' understandings of these and other issues but also contributed to their understandings of geospatial locations relative to the rest of the world. As Brendan shared:

> Well for me, growing up as a kid . . . it seemed like you only use to one thing. Like you're just stuck basically. And I feel like everybody is

stuck and just being in the city. And once I had the opportunity to go to Nashville, Tennessee [to present at a conference on the community garden], to go out, it made me, figure out like, **"Oh!"** Like, I'm missing some stuff out of my life. Like there is a better life out there. It made me want to just step ahead and just reach for a higher goal so I can become more successful and get out and explore and experience things. So, it opened up my mind more, like a lot.

Students' new social networks also included their peers. Angela, a 9th-grader in Ms. Washington's class, captured this important dimension of engaged pedagogies when she noted, "it's just like in the garden . . . it's just like we all were, like, we never talked before, just sitting in the class doing our work. We never really associated with each other." She continued, "suddenly, in the garden, we had to help each other. We had to work together as a class. As a team. So I associated with more people out in the garden than I did before." Both Angela and Brendan point out the value of the following: *Learning together and teamwork. Helping each other. Listening. Caring. Working together.* **Engaged pedagogies**. The *physicalness* of this pedagogy relays to students that their bodies are not sleeves that they take on and off, enter into and out of, or hide and conceal when they approach the classroom door. Instead, their bodies are necessary parts *of* learning, *for* learning, and *in* learning, especially learning that is driven by equity and justice. And their bodies are fine as they are and as they appear.

The types of relational networks made available through engaged pedagogies will differ significantly depending on the design of engagement, the nature of encounters beyond classrooms, and which timescales and landscapes are made available. Recognizing the physical layout, or *physicalness*, of classrooms contained within the walls of schools, as well as the nature of time (class time, school time, and school year), as suggestions in pedagogical endeavors rather than prescriptive boundaries invites us to consider extending and layering space-time to serve engagement and to set into motion just futures. In the expansion of these learningscapes, educators and students are essential rather than exclusive social actors in learning. They collectively open up radical possibilities for teaching and learning *with* families, neighbors, district leaders, and other partners who have an unwavering stake in equity, justice, and the survival of people and communities.

THE PARADOXES OF ENGAGED PEDAGOGIES

We recognize this kind of critically expansive stance toward time and place, and ultimately, learningscapes, as being imaginative, collaborative, and equity-driven processes. We realize that these processes encourage a different rhythm to teaching and learning that emphasize design, fluidity, and improvisation, which can feel counterintuitive to the laser focus of the U.S. public school system on standardization and accountability, which encourages a different rhythm, or perhaps lack of rhythm, because of stasis. This orientation toward learning can lead to playing it safe, which stifles innovation, creativity, and the co-construction of knowledge in real time with students who should be supported to address systemic inequalities.

Tensions might surface for educators adopting engaged pedagogies, as this approach does not play well against corporate standardization and one-size-fits-all accountability measures (see Chapter 1). These tensions represent an epistemic barrier one must deconstruct—rather than a simple hurdle—because the barrier will sit in one's pedagogical field of vision or the field of vision of the leadership in a school. You cannot jump over it, go under it, or move around it. You must break through it. Deconstructing this barrier requires teachers and administrators to collaboratively reflect on the purposes of schooling in a democratic society, the role of education for freedom, and the historic and contemporary positioning of teachers and students on the front lines of social change. Surfacing these deeper purposes and values underneath what Hari (2018) calls "junk values" focused on individualism and materialism allows teachers and administrators to secure their footing on a foundation of engaged pedagogies, equity, and abolitionism.

Organizing learning around the aims of engaged pedagogies as justice work is a more sustainable practice in a field hemorrhaging teachers and students alike who can no longer bear the cost of standardized, routinized learning at the expense of urgent local and global concerns (e.g., survival of Black people in institutions steeped in racist ideologies and white supremacy, a planet suffering from excessive extraction of finite resources, and working people struggling to survive exploitative labor practices). These forces have an erosive effect on teacher recruitment, teacher preparation, and in-service teaching and learning, as well as on our mental, physical, and emotional well-being. Turning toward this more sustainable philosophy rooted in collaboration, equity, and justice can help to repair, heal, energize, and

Protect Black Femmes **by Grace D. Player**

connect teachers, students, families, communities, and schools within (expansive) learningscapes.

The Wellspring

While engaged pedagogies can be generative in terms of space and time, creating a wellspring of energy, creativity, and excitement for students and teachers alike, it can also be tiresome work within the larger context of traditional schools.

"We've been through it," one teacher shared at the end of the school year, after engaging with her students around several projects.

"We don't emphasize teaching as engagement that leads to and that really is equity," another teacher explained.

"My students loved walking to the community space to learn with elders and learn together," reflected another teacher.

There was a lack of support, including insufficient materials and funds, in some of the schools where BLTL educators worked. There was also lackluster policy and structures needed to sustain the work. The rigidity of these environments and the absence of necessary structures can create a tension—an exhausting tension, in fact—for teachers who engage in this work. Long-range visions collide with the more immediate formative and summative assessments confronting teachers. Working alongside students in community happens while stacks of papers are piling up in need of grading. In our pursuit of engaged pedagogies with students, teachers, and community partners, we are aware that systemic, structural, and cultural barriers can become a well in which we pour our energies and that can prevent the work from being fully realized. While we are committed to creating the conditions necessary for engaged pedagogies as justice teaching and learning, we are also aware, as we write in Chapter 1, that this work can only be sustainable within environments that have been, or are willing to be, reimagined, refigured, and rebuilt.

We name these tensions to put the barriers in view. Naming the issues BLTL educators faced is the first step to addressing them. No longer cast as the background, as the fixed set on the stage on which we teach and learn, they are instead cast as suspect, anachronistic, and out of place for the kind of work we are being tasked to do in this very moment. Engaged pedagogies have a way of setting into motion an experience of encounter between scripted worlds and imaginative worlds, wordy worlds and worldly words, and among students, teachers and community partners. Such encounters can generate a life source for restoration and justice. A strength and challenge of engaged pedagogies is this generative nature—what is learned cannot necessarily be predetermined. When this work is set against a backdrop of standardization and accountability, it becomes problematic. As Ms. Reed shared, students are "learning gratitude, empathy—they're marketable skills, but they aren't going to give them the test score." Set against a much deeper, historicized, perhaps yet-to-be-realized backdrop of schools as sites of democratic participation, the generative nature of engaged pedagogies rooted in collaboration, equity, and abolitionism is promising. Thus, we recognize that this work is truly sustainable if it occurs within new structures of justice teaching and learning that are imaginative and creative.

Tanya, Angela, and Kristopher, three students (among others) we reference throughout this chapter, remind us to "Think outside the box" **(Tanya)**; to "Think outside of just English, Math, Science, and get more involved in your students outside of class because there are so many opportunities that are there for them" **(Angela)**; and to understand the importance of "having like the community that surrounds your school work together to do something creative in the neighborhood" **(Kristopher)**.

IMPROVISATION ARTISTS, MASTERFUL WEAVERS

We anticipate the stories shared in this chapter will resonate with many educators who are committed to humanizing relationships with students and, like BLTL educators, who courageously and dynamically shape learning opportunities in classrooms that prioritize students' needs. Teachers work within the constraints of larger political economies that have failed to fully prioritize the learning of children and youth (see *Williams v. Reeves*, *Gary B. v. Snyder*, and *Ella T. v. State of California*) and the lives of teachers (e.g., strikes leading into the 2019–2020 school year; concerns with in-person teaching during a pandemic). BLTL educators have established or have quickly developed a level of comfort with improvisation by responding to the emergent qualities of engaged pedagogies. This includes the emergent nature of our lives, realities, and ideas born out of encounter, exploration, and dialogue.

They are masterful weavers who thread together timescales and geographies in order to nurture student motivation and facilitate student growth. Through this process, they reveal again and again the interdependent nature of public schools, communities, and families.

They showcase how historical lessons are connected to matters of justice and abolitionist visions of futures. The efforts of BLTL educators are vital to the work of the current moment and the future, which calls us to simultaneously account for the democratic and moral imagination of public schools for what they should be: sites of learning, equity, justice, and freedom.

"Really Not Waiting": Our Found Poem #6

Offered by Valerie, Emily, Tamara, and Grace

Waiting for what?
Engaged pedagogies and
Justice work.
As invitations to:
Think
Dream
Live
Exist Whole
and
Love whole
And
Be whole
Within learningscapes
With Irradicable impacts.
Working for equity
Moving toward justice.

Really not waiting.

CHAPTER 6

Irradicable Impacts
Engaged Pedagogies as Invitations to Equitable Learningscapes

During BLTL, an ethic of mutuality, responsibility, and care rippled through the school district and its many communities. Collaboration among teachers, students, and community members generated a beautiful, entangled web of human lives. As educators reimagined their teaching, and as other participants reframed their interactions and rooted their conversations in love and diverse abilities, we bore witness to a current of trust, respect, and change surging through classrooms and communities. Seeing this type of reenergizing, we thought about teaching, learning, and engagement that centered what AnaLouise Keating (2013) calls "our radical interconnectedness" (p. 178). For Keating, radical interconnectedness challenges individualistic, self-centered, possessive, me-consciousness tendencies associated with Western cultures, and promotes an inclusive, interwoven, we-consciousness with both human and nonhuman life, insisting that "we are both distinct individuals and integral parts of a series of larger wholes" (p. 177).

Activists Ella Baker and Angela Davis remind us that radical means "by the root." In their approaches to social justice, both Davis and Baker were attentive to not only the needs of everyday people on the ground, but also to how those needs extended deep into the soil as longstanding forms of inequities, injustices, and oppressions. They were keenly aware of how the need for voting rights, accessible and equitable education, prison abolition, and fair living wages, among other things, impacted lives beyond local communities. Their philosophies and actions spoke to an understanding of society as an ecosystem or, as we refer to it in Chapter 5, a learningscape, held together by an underground network of interwoven histories, nourished by respect, love, and communication, capable of producing large yields of justice, joy, and equity. Therefore, if we want things to flourish (e.g., joy, justice, and equity), then we need to reengage and support all parts of the learningscape.

BLTL offered an invitation for all to reevaluate their roles in this ecological system, and to consider how we can collectively reengage for justice, joy, and equity. Schools were invited to participate in this initiative in order to holistically reengage in the lives of children—Black children, Children of Color, and white children from poor and working-class backgrounds. Families, community leaders, teachers, and teachers' union members were invited to reengage in the soul of schools, which were called to reengage *with* and *in* communities. Students, guardians, caregivers, school administrators, and educators were invited to conceptualize and participate in intergenerational engagements. Such practices ignited previously foreclosed pathways and moved us closer to an irradicable ecosystem, where each person and institution became responsible and responsive to one another. In the spirit of mutuality and shared responsibility, the BLTL initiative did not task children, youth, and families *alone* with doing more. It did not shoulder teachers or school administrators with the burdensome responsibility of implementing yet one more unfunded, under-supported mandate. The invitation was cast wide, and the sentiment was ubiquitous: engaged pedagogies are most impactful when students, educators, and communities connect with, talk to, learn from, and rely on one another.

In extending an invitation to teaching and learning rooted in these ideals, BLTL merged into the historical company of other initiatives that have sought to stress the *public* in public schooling and realize the promise of this social institution in the democratic landscape of the United States. Invitations of considerable historic weight have emphasized a shared sense of unity, cooperation, organization, and cultural analysis (Freire, 1970/2000) key to any cultural shift(s) in consciousness. From *Brown v. Board of Education* and the Elementary and Secondary Education Act of 1965 to the work of students and teachers fighting anti-Blackness and COVID-19 in 2020 and beyond,[1] we see what is possible when people are allotted time and space to come together in meaningful ways to lay bare, interrogate, and propose solutions to issues impacting all of our lives, neighborhoods, and futures.

RÉPONDEZ S'IL VOUS PLAÎT: AN INVITATION

As we describe in other chapters, BLTL generated pathways that promoted encounters among people wanting healthy, hopeful, and whole public and collective futures. Participants across the district came to the initiative with a shared understanding that those futures are cultivated by engagement apprentices who are committed to

> Creating and protecting ecosystems of **learning**;
> Pursuing **justice** through creative inquiry; and
> Working across generations for **equity**.

In this chapter, we offer brief scenes from BLTL as openings where invitations were extended at the level of family (among siblings), of classmates (among peers), and of colleagues (between teachers and families). These scenes illustrate that within the unifying framework of engagement, there were many uncommon occurrences at the interpersonal level that were significant to our work that we did not anticipate and for which we could not have planned.

Sometimes, the ordinary, interpersonal occurrences are overlooked in partnerships of this size, especially if collaborators are in pursuit of generalizable outcomes for district-level reporting, grant requirements, desired replication, major curricular shifts, or other matters of scale. We have come to better *embrace* this notion of scale because in matters of equity and justice, we need humanizing antiracist policies, programs, and pedagogies to not only spread quickly and widely, but to be sustained within systems and institutions. Simultaneously, we temper our embrace of scale, particularly if it means losing sight of the impactful stories shared with us from others—stories that proved to be integral to refiguring schooling, reimagining teaching and learning, and reinvigorating expressions of engagement in this work. Some of these stories capture the spirit of organizing that happened among BLTL participants in ways that understand community organizing as the heart of true social change. For Garza (2020), community organizing is "the messy work of bringing people together, from different backgrounds and experiences, to change the conditions they are living in." She continues, "It is the work of building relationships among people who may believe they have nothing in common so that together they can achieve a common goal" (p. 57). These relationships and the *experiences* of relationship-building were foundational not just to BLTL but, equally importantly, to the work that children, youth, educators, families, community members, and researchers do throughout their lives in contending with power and fighting for justice.

We hope that by highlighting these intimate and underexplored connections, we can illustrate their importance in projects of justice as well as the inherent dangers that arise if we ignore, unintentionally dismiss, and intentionally erase them through stories only about scale.

The kinds of change desired by BLTL are about subtle shifts in consciousness, connectedness, and shared responsibility at the *relational* level (Keating, 2013). Subtle shifts help us account for our response to the question Dian Marino (1998) asked about her own work: "How do we know if we're engaged in producing truly emancipatory materials, or if we're only reproducing colonized patterns" (p. 103)? How do we ensure that we open up, rather than circumscribe what Ariel Dorfman (1996) describes as our "freedom not only to become another person, but also to invent another kind of world" (as cited in Marino, p. 104)? To answer these questions, we engage the "radical interconnectedness," or the roots of BLTL, to hear how students, educators, communities, and other participants responded to our invitation to teach and learn differently. Through their intimate, quotidian practices, we learn more about interpersonal inquiry—learning about self and others—as a route to collective emancipation and inventions of freedom.

SCENE I: SISTERS' ORGANIC LEARNINGSCAPES

"I didn't realize she was doing this in her school, too," Chika confessed as she watched her sister offer a presentation at the BLTL symposium.[2] Standing between classmates from Vanguard Academy and the school's guidance counselor, Aneesa (Chika's sister) shared the inner workings of the group's BLTL project that they named, "Stories Behind Their Eyes." Each group member wore a fluorescent orange T-shirt, which matched the color of their flyers. According to the group, they dedicated time to post their flyers at local rest areas and truck stops across the city, and they included details about signs of human sex trafficking and contact information of agencies that help survivors. Students, teachers, legislators, and invited guests listened intently as Aneesa spoke about the group's efforts to raise awareness about trafficking as a local, national, and global issue.

"Stories Behind Their Eyes" was a multifaceted project that focused on learning from survivors, sharing their stories of resilience, and finding ways to interrupt the trafficking cycle. Vanguard Academy's students and guidance counselor were working with a premonition. During the writing of this book, news broke about one of the largest human trafficking stings in the history of this midwestern state—with more than 170 people arrested and more than 100 survivors rescued. The premonition was surging through the district and city, and pulsated into a network of sisters.

Sisters by Grace D. Player

As a 9th-grade student at Justice High School, Chika was focused on taking notes on the presentation for extra credit. Although she and Aneesa live together, they attended different schools, and this public presentation seemed to be the first time that she heard her older sister talk about the "Stories Behind Their Eyes" project or human sex trafficking. Earlier in the year, Chika and her classmates were tasked with developing a Social Justice Capstone project for their World Humanities class (see Chapter 4). The teachers shared student-generated videos, posters, and photos from the capstone projects from years prior. As we describe in Chapter 4, 9th-graders tackled issues of homelessness, gentrification, bullying, animal rights, and human sex trafficking. In an interview with Chika and the three other girls in her group, one of them shared that they chose the topic after watching a short film that a previous group wrote, filmed, edited, and submitted as a class assignment. The story line follows: When a family faces a financial crisis and possible eviction, the daughter looks for work. In replying to what appears to be a legitimate job posting, she is kidnapped and forced into the world of human trafficking. The daughter sees a flyer, similar to those that Aneesa's group later created and distributed, and makes a phone call. With the help of the agency and police, she is reunited with her family. The film ends with a caveat: Not every trafficking story is this neat and linear—as some trafficked individuals do not survive, while there are others who are still missing.

Chika and her classmates took a different approach to the topic. Instead of a film, they created an art piece deeply influenced by her sister's project. When Chika learned that she and Aneesa are fighting the same injustice, the fissure between their schools and projects began to close. In attending more Vanguard Academy–sponsored events with Aneesa, Chika's work with classmates at Justice High became more layered and nuanced. For example, when Vanguard Academy sponsored an author talk with a trafficking survivor who also wrote about her experiences, Chika attended and was able to listen to an interview with the author. During their work on their capstone project at Justice High, Chika shared with her group her insights and artifacts from the event, which included her notes, various pamphlets, readings, and flyers.

For the final project, Chika and her team paid homage to the connection BLTL helped to foster. The group of girls submitted a large art piece of multiple hands of various complexions, which represented, according to the group, "different ethnics and genders" of people impacted by human trafficking. To complicate our understandings of perpetrators and survivors, they painted red and purple markings on each of the hands. For them, the "Stories Behind Their Hands" were multifaceted, urgent, and complex lessons they learned from their research and engagements with Vanguard Academy's "Stories Behind Their Eyes" project. For us, Chika and Aneesa demonstrate how justice-centered inquiry can generate organic learningscapes for students and families. With the desire to interrupt and end human sex trafficking, both siblings used their classrooms, communities, and home spaces to interrogate the issue, connect with one another, and launch an awareness campaign across two schools in the district.

SCENE II: ENGAGING FRATERNAL PROXIMITIES

Todd and Benjamin, brothers who attended Liberty High School, both excelled when it came to engaged forms of learning. Neither liked school, and they had both honed some of their persuasive skills by mounting arguments to their parents about why they did not need to go to school on particular days of the week. When it came to Ms.

Washington's class, however, they were fully engaged. In fact, it was Ms. Washington's class that kept Todd and Benjamin's family at Liberty High School. While their family lived in a different district, their mother used the open enrollment policy of Liberty High to keep them close to Ms. Washington and within the dynamic learning environment she had created for students.

Two years apart in grade and age, Benjamin had trailed Todd throughout their schooling. For the most part, their experiences remained

> *Separate. Different.* **Disconnected one from the other.** *Distinct.*

It was in Ms. Washington's class where their academic and engaged lives collided. Todd, who had joined the Design Team[3] as a freshman, welcomed Benjamin when he enrolled in the school. Todd knew this would be the right kind of learning for his brother, an ELA class that encouraged action alongside deep, analytic thought, and that invited students to pose questions about the world around them and to explore connections between language arts and their communities. As we discuss in previous chapters, students prepared grant proposals to secure materials for a wheelchair-accessible community garden. They also used creative writing to envision *who* the garden might bring together and *how*. And they designed multimodal flyers and trifold posters to encourage their peers and other teachers to root out ableist language from their vocabulary and to question how notions of "normal" had unfortunately taken hold of their worldviews.

Todd was right. Benjamin loved Ms. Washington's class and participated in community engaged learning. According to Benjamin, "Sometimes I'll just go like, 'I can't believe I did this much in my freshman year.' This is the best writing, best Language Arts class I've ever had."

Ms. Washington's class received positive attention from local news organizations, and her work was highly respected by her building principal, who supported her teaching approaches and forms of engagements with students. In fact, the engaged practices and efforts of Ms. Washington, her students, and their community partners also earned them an invitation to several local and national conferences where students were invited to talk about their learning. One such conference, organized by the BLTL initiative, put Todd and Benjamin side by side on a public stage.

Image designed by Brian Kellett

"I got really nervous," Benjamin recalled, "in front of the 30 or 40 at the Audubon Center." By contrast, Benjamin noticed, was his brother Todd. "When my brother was speaking, he made, he actually made a woman cry." Todd's playful disposition, which more often resulted in laughter from a crowd than regard, captured the reverence of both the audience and his younger brother alike. Benjamin settled into a calm demeanor as he witnessed the admiration a large group of people had for his brother's captivating presentation about the community garden and disability awareness campaign in which they participated. Witnessing his brother engage with an audience offered Benjamin the kind of experience he needed to prepare for his own upcoming presentations, to refine his strategies accordingly, and to have agency in how he would come to think about his own learning. In a follow-up discussion with Benjamin, he shared, "I'm speaking in Atlanta, Georgia . . . and then I'm speaking in June in front of 300 principals." He was invited, with some of his peers and his brother, to discuss the impact the BLTL initiative had on his learning and engagement at a National Education Association (NEA) convening. He was excited by the opportunity to travel to Atlanta for various reasons. His mother was born there, and having never visited the place where she navigated girlhood drew him to Atlanta, as it was layered with not only a school-based assignment (presenting on BLTL) but also familial desires (to learn more about his mother).

Todd and Benjamin, like other sibling pairings, were already experiencing a "sticky" proximity (Davies, 2019) by attending the same school, and they were only 2 years a part. They influenced one another's social and academic engagements by way of their biological connection, which often established expectations from their respective teachers and peers. Having had one brother in class, a teacher might anticipate the sibling would behave and engage in similar ways. The "rubbing off" and "soaking in," to borrow phrases from Davies

(2019), of a sibling's approach to schooling, life, and, in this particular case, public speaking, was an opening that captured our attention. However, this opening often went underexplored because these dynamics were rapidly unfolding in intimate spaces such as within Todd and Benjamin's homes, where we did not have access. We remain intrigued by their evolution and interconnectedness within school, local and national communities, and inside their home, knowing that the potential power of sibling support (Davies, 2019) often surfaced within Liberty High School and that it might continue to emerge down the proverbial road if these brothers live elsewhere. We are intrigued by shifts in space and time, as discussed in Chapter 5, because many of them were fundamental to how Todd and Benjamin strategically collaborated to design and support the goals, purposes, and priorities of the disability awareness campaign and the community garden on local, regional, and national stages.

SCENE III: ENGAGEMENT AS RETENTION

Ms. Mulvihill worked as a colleague of Ms. Washington's at Liberty High School. She taught 10th- and 11th-grade ELA and, like Ms. Washington, operated with a spirit of engagement well before she joined the BLTL initiative. Through BLTL, however, she further strengthened her skills and became better connected with other teachers in her school and across the district who were doing the work of engaged pedagogies such as justice teaching and learning.

One spring afternoon during their teacher preparation period, we were talking with Ms. Washington and Ms. Mulvihill, and the conversation quickly turned toward an underlying antithesis of engagement:

Disengagement.
DISENGAGEMENT!

We were surrounded by empty desks in Ms. Mulvihill's classroom, given that the early departure of students was symbolically expressed by the empty desks and chairs. Ms. Mulvihill's point was magnified by the fact that approximately 1,600 students across the district departed before graduation, with many of them having been pushed out before completing school. In fact, when both Ms. Washington and Ms. Mulvihill referenced ongoing disconnections among young people and school, we dove in.

"I mean I try so hard, I will literally [search for] you . . . anywhere. Last year I did lose a kid. Four years ago, I lost a kid. You remember . . ." *and Ms. Mulvihill lips a name to Ms. Washington who nods her head in remembrance and agreement.*

Ms. Mulvihill continued, "I went and found him and brought him back, and he came back for a couple of weeks, and then he was just gone. And sometimes kids just don't, they just have so much." A veteran educator well aware of the humanitarian crisis facing many of our young people and their families, Ms. Mulvihill developed short-range strategies that helped her to navigate the more immediate demands of working toward justice with longer-range plans, expressed through engaged pedagogies. One of her short-range strategies, however unconventional it was, involved her very own minivan. She would drive around, look for, talk with, and agree to transport students and families. Sometimes, as she said, it would be to transport students to school. She was known across the district as an educator who understood that the timescales of school did not always map onto the city's bus schedules or the availability of family members or friends with cars. She confessed to us that sometimes the minivan was used to take students to athletic competitions or to drop them off at home.

Ms. Mulvihill's longer-range strategy, engaged pedagogies, allowed her to attend to more systemic issues threatening the lives of young people, as discussed in Chapter 1. She simultaneously facilitated with students several engaged projects out of her classroom and through her curricula. Some of these included a tutoring program with a local elementary school, an anti-bullying awareness campaign, suicide prevention, and Cans for the Canopy; the latter was dedicated to global environmental awareness and protection. Each of these projects were selected because they tied into students' lives and because students saw the interconnected nature of the problems facing our communities: mentoring connected to social isolation connected to suicide connected to environmental devastation. These were all connected for students—by pain, urgency, and a sense of responsibility—and they hoped that school, and in this case, through their ELA class, would help them to better connect the dots.

Ms. Mulvihill explained, "the nice thing is that the kids bring stuff to you. I think ideally, you know, you're taking, you're incorporating something that's outside of the typical, the sphere of typical school and you're incorporating it into the classroom and well beyond, and also, incorporating, weaving it through the curriculum." She continued:

> Or pointing out where the curriculum touches it so you're strengthening it. You may have already been reading *Ceremony* by Leslie Marman Soco,

but now you're saying, 'okay, look at the, you know, look at the environmental implications of this, and what's happening to the land there. And think about this,' you know? Or you might have already been looking at Nobel Prize winners, but now you can directly take Wangari Maathai or, Muhammad Yunus, you know, or Michael Banking and figure out ways that that could be used in other countries and apply it.

One project emerged from another.

She continued: "And then the bullying . . . came up on its own with the kids and that's actually branched out so that I've had three 10th-graders come to me and say, 'well maybe we should start an anti-suicide component that next year.' And I said, 'Okay.' I'm willing to consider that." Ms. Mulvihill's students sought connection, and she responded. She designed learning around issues students cared deeply about, asked to investigate further, and eagerly responded to in their learning and engagement with each other. Many of the students' families noticed, too, because the projects mattered to them and they responded. Ms. Mulvihill remembered one mother who had "continued to collect cans even though [her son] is not in my class. . . . I've had a couple moms and they'll see me somewhere, wherever, Meijer [grocery store] or wherever, 'Oh my God, I have been carrying these cans for three months. I can't even put any groceries away" *[Ms. Mulvihill moves her hands around, similar to how the mothers had moved theirs as they talked, gesturing toward the trunk of their cars]*. For us, we see this as impactful learning that was cultivated from engaged pedagogies and the deep connections that grew among students, their families, and Ms. Mulvihill.

SCENE IV: REALLY . . . A POWER DRILL?

It was a level three lockdown. **It was a drill.** Gunman in the building. We moved to the back of the classroom along with all of the students, Mr. Spears (the preservice teacher who was delivering a lesson on haikus), and Ms. Washington (the classroom teacher).

Mr. Spears, a master of education student at a nearby college, was fully immersed in his student-teaching experience in Ms. Washington's classroom. He was watching, studying, and developing new skills and methods based on Ms. Washington's engaged pedagogical approach to 9th-grade literature and ELA. He was also beginning to teach his own lessons and was receiving constructive feedback from Ms. Washington. Then suddenly came—

> Get away from the window.
> **Move away from the door!**
> Be quiet. Whatever you do, don't move.

If there had been a gunman in the building, according to the lockdown procedure, the above directives would allegedly keep everyone inside safe.

Ms. Washington was in charge of closing and locking the door. Turning off the lights. And then joining her students and Mr. Spears . . . in silence.

> The first part of the drill lasted 15 long minutes.

According to Everytown's report titled, *Gunfire on School Grounds*, there were a total of 51 incidents of gunfire in 2013 across K–12 school and universities/colleges, resulting in 26 deaths, of which six were death by suicide (Everytown, 2019). That same year, the U.S. Senate rejected an expansion of universal background checks (Barrett & Cohen, 2013). Until this country and its elected leaders are willing to enact a policy that makes the influences of organizations such as the NRA unlawful, this kind of unethical entanglement between private power and government makes these drills appear to be a sensible way to spend schooltime (we do not think they are).

> Then came a loud knock at the classroom door. One of desperation. Lots of desperation!

In a terrifying layering of familiarity and fable, the principal's voice pierced the solid wooden door, "Let me in, let me in, by the hair of my chinny chin chin!"

> He was playing the role of the gunman.

An assistant principal, playing the part of herself, was in the *same* hallway as the alleged gunman. Minutes later, the assistant principal began appealing to the silent group in the classroom for help:

> "Help! Let me in! I need in!"

Irradicable Impacts

She banged on the door, wiggled the handle, and then there was quiet. Nothing moved.

The students, who had been chattering before the state-sanctioned simulation of terror designed to prepare them for federal negligence around gun control, echoed her silence.

A few minutes later, one of the administrators came over the loudspeaker and announced to the entire school, *"The drill is over."*

We all began moving back to where we had been before. The room, once again, came alive with student chatter, and Mr. Spears shuffled his papers to determine what he could reasonably cover in the remaining 10 minutes of class.

Ms. Washington looked around, leaned over, and whispered to a few of us present that day. She shared that she thought for a level-three lockdown that the principal was supposed to come around and unlock the doors to signal the drill was over. Not announce it.

WE ARE STILL IN THE SIMULATION!

The principal's voice came over the loudspeaker. He declared, *"No one should be moving!* In the event of an active shooter, it could have been the gunman, forcing the principal at gunpoint, to prompt teachers to unlock their doors."

No one move! So everyone in the classroom froze. Still.

Then, we all migrated to the back of the room quietly. We sat for another 5 very long and very quiet minutes.

We finally heard the sound of metal on metal, as the door, which needs a key to be locked and unlocked from both the outside and the inside, turned over, marking the end of the preservice teacher's lesson with students on haikus, generally, as well as all of our own larger traumatic lessons about the real systems-level violence threatening schools, specifically.

The drill was done. We sat there wondering: Why would it be reasonable to think that the gunman was clever enough to force someone to use the loudspeaker to persuade everyone in the building to unlock their doors, but somehow beyond the scope of this terrifying drill, he would not also consider stealing someone's keys to get in?

An engaged framework surfaces in this very moment as significant because of its potential to give way to learningscapes—to invite Mr. Spears, in particular, to consider the influences of private interests on his future classrooms and how engaged pedagogies might serve him as a future teacher. The following were also under consideration:

- Legislative timescales that backdrop active shooter drills in schools, including the painfully and deathly slow move toward universal background checks (Everytown, n.d.)
- Ways to invite students to interrogate why these drills exist, whose agendas they serve, and what the alternatives might be
- Why young people are portrayed as violent, and their schools as sites of violence rather than exposing the root causes of the violence

> Children still dying
> in their sanctums. All their lives
> bleeding out in lead (Li Sui, 2018)

SCENE V: AN INVITATION TO RECLAIM OUR FUTURES

Chiara Francesca, Chicago-based "acupuncturist, organizer, artist immigrant and former teen parent living with a disability," brings us back to thinking about our role in cultivating futures and ecosystems, or learningscapes, that are equitable and just, and that lead to freedom. According to Francesca (2020):

> and also
> this year has given us, as a species, so many opportunities for learning
> for clearly discerning what ideologies, institutions, behaviors and paradigms do not serve us
> and for the chance to intentionally choose the seeds we need planting

Francesca also reminds us that:

> we will seed better worlds
> we will grow just futures (Francesca, 2020)

In order to think deeply about learningscapes, we must put our hands in the soil of today, which is still tainted with injustice, inequities, and oppressive ideologies. We must yearn for futures that are built with joy, respect, and mutuality. The previous scenes are nodes in a network of teachers, students, families, and community leaders. They are openings in the web of justice-oriented, community-centered projects that demonstrate links across learningscapes that are experienced as engaged pedagogies. Such links reveal spaces and places of equity where teachers and students relearn their powers to connect and reimagine new worlds and ways of being, even in the unfortunate presence of looming threats of school violence and realities of exploitation that threaten personhood and freedom. BLTL students and educators illustrate what warrior poet and philosopher Audre Lorde gleaned years ago: "at the edge of each other's battle, the war is the same" (Abod, 2002).

Thus, it is our responsibility to pause and listen to one another, and to place our fingers on the pulse of what is deeply impacting and intriguing our students, colleagues, teachers, families, neighbors, and administrators. For us, engaged pedagogies summon us to the ground. Engaged pedagogies require that we be present and open. Engaged pedagogies ask that we gather around the granular experiences between siblings in order to make sense of larger movements toward justice. We are called to remember that these moments are concurrent with classroom practices, societal shifts, and lived realities. We understand engagement as embodied practices. As a result, learning is iterative and intimate. No two students or teachers approached their projects and justice work the same. By combatting the threat and realty of human sex trafficking, for example, Chika and Aneesa forged connections in their homes, in their schools, and across an entire district.

If these invitations and openings can generate connections for students, what kinds of openings were generated for teachers? In a hostile sociopolitical climate, Ms. Washington and Ms. Mulvihill connected and created spaces for Todd and Benjamin to both imagine and codesign learning connections. Although the teachers at Vanguard Academy and Justice High School did not work together, their projects created an underground network for learning. These engagements also sent another pulse of energy through the district as educators began to harness their own visions for more equitable futures, especially as they learned from their students.

BLTL educators wanting to "seed better worlds" saw themselves doing so from a different vantage point. Although they enjoyed teaching, some of them, especially those who also worked closely with undergraduate and graduate university students, expressed an interest in returning to school for doctoral degrees. One of the World Humanities teachers at Justice High School, Mr. Merry, was pursuing (and successfully completed) a doctorate while teaching and formulating social justice curricula for the district. After his participation in BLTL, one of

***Roots & Seeds* by Grace D. Player**

his colleagues, Mrs. Penn, entered a doctoral program at a local university and recently earned her doctorate degree. Other BLTL educators took their desires for equity into their work with teachers, as Ms. Washington began working with one of the largest teachers' unions (following her years of service to the union, she recently returned to the classroom) and Ms. Reed (a former middle school teacher) currently serves as a literacy coach at a local high school. As they each inspired students to see themselves as leaders and change makers, they also cultivated their own leadership capacities and sensibilities. They inspire us!

BLTL continues, embedded in a larger ecosystem, or learningscape, of equity. There are some nodes that we cannot and did not see. Students have matriculated out of the K–12 classrooms and into the larger world. Some teachers are still working, but others are no longer working in the school district. However, it is possible that we are all still carrying pieces of this work with us, and that it manifests in our teaching, learning, engagements, and everyday politics. The key to justice work is living in the spaces of unknowingness and uncertainty, as growth is unpredictable, yet inevitable. And within these spaces, remaining unwavering in our commitments to equity, justice, and freedom. As we each geographically relocate(d) to places outside of the original BLTL sites, we did so with intention to connection. We imagine that each family, student, teacher, community partner, and administrator is still linked into the intricate web of dreamers and world builders, sharing stories of joy, strategies for reciprocity, and visions of mutuality. We see them on social media. We chat with them via email. We hold tight to the lessons they afforded us.

We each stand with a discerning readiness at our nodes in the web waiting for, and with, invitations to continue teaching and learning that engage, connect, and move us closer to more just and equitable futures.

With these things in mind, we end this chapter with a few questions for you to consider:

- What scenes from your own teaching and learning have you witnessed among students? How are these scenes embedded in engagement and equity/equity-as-engagement?
- How do you take up radical interconnectedness in your teaching and learning?
- How do commitments to equity, justice, and freedom appear and reappear, over and over again, in your teaching and learning?
- How do they appear and reappear in your interactions with students?
- How about in your interactions with families and communities?
- Are you still asking, "Where is the Justice?" Are you still waiting for justice? Or are you actively pursuing it? **HOW?**

"Moving, Even in Stillness": Our Found Poem #7

Offered by Valerie, Emily, Tamara, and Grace

Still waiting
For what?
Engaged pedagogies and
Justice work.
For equity and freedom
For our learning to liberate us
In communities
Of hope
Of belonging
Of transformation.
In schools
And
In the world.
Refusing to
Continue to
Wait . . .
For what?

We move
Even
In stillness.

CHAPTER 7

Waiting for What?

> For women, then, poetry is not a luxury. It is a vital necessity of our existence. It forms the quality of the light within which we predicate our hopes and dreams toward survival and change, first made into language, then into idea, then into more tangible action (Lorde, 1984, p. 37).

> Feminist researchers reveal—or revel in—the situatedness of knowledge claims through the practice of reflexivity (Ohito & Nyachae, 2019, p. 841).

In late Fall 2020, we gathered together on Zoom, as we had regularly done throughout the writing of this book, to discuss what this last chapter would look like in *Where Is the Justice? Engaged Pedagogies in Schools and Communities*. We were, without question, not only committed to completing this book, but, more importantly, to maintaining our practice of being in community with each other—wherever, whenever, and however we appeared. As on all other occasions, our faces popped up on our computer screens. Our smiles and laughter instantly released us from the busyness of the colliding dynamics of home and work. We were temporarily removed from whatever else was occupying our minds, bodies, and souls. Without hesitation, our laughter turned into unplanned outbursts, semi-dry but equally funny jokes, tangentially off-topic soliloquies, and smart-mouthed comments about how family members were in the background watching "Let's Make a Deal." References to trying to purchase new eyeglasses without having enough money in the flexible spending account were followed by our worries about how Black, Indigenous, Latinx, and other People of Color would survive and thrive in the face of a raging global pandemic. *What about children? Young adults? Families? Teachers? Artists? Activists? Communities of Color?*

> These wonderings always led us into a discussion about reimagining public education.

Valerie by Grace D. Player

Emily by Grace D. Player

Waiting for What?

Grace by Grace D. Player

Tamara by Grace D. Player

On this particular morning, we continued our practice of *being in relation* by listening to, talking with, and learning from each other. For example, we shared aspects of our personal and professional lives in the same breath that we discussed the current conditions of U.S. public education. Embedded in our exchanges were also explicit references to the horrifying state of the country, the pandemic, remote teaching and learning with students and teachers in under-resourced communities, and the never-ending reality of racial violence endured by many People of Color. Our focus always returned to engaged pedagogies: What are some of the lessons, implications, and promises of such pedagogies within schools and communities? How can engaged pedagogies help us frame and name why the country, by and large, was still **not** antiracist? Was still **not** anti-oppressive? Was undergoing an insurrection on the U.S. Capitol? Why and how would engaged pedagogies be useful in our work for equity and because of justice inside schools, in communities, and around the world? What would it take for engaged pedagogies to lead to a reimagining and rebuilding of schools? Would engaged pedagogies center love and joy, criticality and humanity, youth and families, communities and society, over corporatized, standardized efforts for "compliance" over equity, equality, justice, and opportunity?

These questions, among many others, continue to motivate our work, whether we are revisiting data from the BLTL initiative, teaching preservice teacher education students, collaborating on sustainable community-engaged projects, enacting a model of transformative leadership in practice, or working to build just communities with educators and activists. We are committed to this work, and we hope you will join us to center engaged pedagogies in theory and practice, in school and communities.

THIS IS NOT AN ENDING

So, where do we go from here? How do we make sense of the lessons we learned from BLTL students, educators, and collaborators, along with the questions that are still lingering, waiting to be answered? As we continue to think through these questions, it seems only fitting that we end this book not with a traditional ending or a goodbye, but with a creative beginning, an opening.

A found poem!

The following found poem came into being because we (Valerie, Emily, Tamara, and Grace) were willing to be vulnerable with each other. We shared our thoughts, fears, and hopes for what engaged pedagogies and justice work should mean within schools and communities by focusing on, to borrow Emily's words, "human dignity." We also talked about being committed to "relationships and being in relation to" students, teachers, and families, as Tamara expressed. This idea connected to Grace's desire to always work toward "relationships, trust, and agency," and to Valerie's commitment to "center love" in teaching and learning.

From our words, our found poem came into its written design because of Valerie's proclivity for found poetry, and it came into artistic being because of Grace's creative brilliance. We offer it here, not simply as a way to close this book, but as an invitation into understanding, as Audre Lorde (1984) tells us, that poetry "is a vital necessity of our existence" that allows us the space and time to "predicate our hopes and dreams toward survival and change" (p. 37). We hope you will read, study, engage in "the practice of reflexivity" (Ohito & Nyachae, 2019, p. 841), and center engaged pedagogies to productively answer our guiding question, "Where Is the Justice?" and the subquestion that emerged, "Waiting for What?"

"Waiting for What?" An Offering Found in Poetry (#8)

Understanding engaged pedagogies as:
Connections to others
Expansive uptakes of literacies
Collaborations and partnerships.
And these are all grounded in *and* guided by
Equity *and*
Justice *and*
Love *and*
Freedom *and*
Our humanity.

We are connected
One with another *and*
In relation to
Families *and*
Students *and*
Teachers *and*
Administrators *and*
Communities and schools.
Everywhere where people are
Where learning and engagement happen.

Understanding engaged pedagogies as:
Painting stories about
Human dignity and human lives.
With integrity and grace
We commit to being in right relation *and*
Responsive and responsible *to* and *for* and *with*
Others and ourselves—those here and those yet to be here.
We foster relationships *and*
Envision and enact teaching *as* learning *as* doing *as*
Living *as* being *as* vulnerable *as* surviving *as* thriving . . . together.

Because we commit to breaking down barriers between
Researchers and practitioners *and*
Students and teachers
In order to create and sustain relationships of trust

In and *for* trust
Because of trust and *through* trust
In how we learn with and from children and young people *and*
Community leaders and educators *and*
Families and activists and advocates.
To create new meanings of teaching as justice, learning as liberation.

Understanding engaged pedagogies to:
Examine racial violence *and*
Dismantle systems of racial injustices.
To reimagine, refigure, and rebuild schools
Into spaces of love, joy, inquiry, and learning
Through intergenerational learning *and*
Transformative engagements
That situate teaching not as
Distance/distant to, separate/separated from, or siloed/territorial within.
But as imaginative, valued, loving, humanizing, necessary, revolutionary.

Engaged pedagogies as embodied practices
Recognize that many of us
Live in spaces of unknowingness and uncertainty,
That are enraptured with violence and oppression.
And so let it be that engaged pedagogies
Provide openings for us to confront, name, and heal from trauma and pain,
As we teach justice *and* move toward freedom
For our individual and collective well-being *and*
For our liberated lives now in our present state
And for our liberated lives well into our futures.

Waiting for what?
Is neither an option nor a luxury.
Students can no longer wait for us to
Decide to reform schooling systems . . . again,
And to maybe get it right this time or wrong . . . again.
We cannot ask students to forgive us . . . again.
Because we have chosen to not understand . . . again
"Teaching to transgress" and "education as a practice of freedom."[1]

We should never expect students, families, and communities
To forgive us for oppressing them and neglecting their dreams and desires.

We must trouble our assumptions about
What we think we are doing *for*
Students and families
By talking and listening to them *and*
Willingly learning with, about, and from them too.
We must resist the tendency to think
That we are saving them
We are not!
They are leading us, only if we will listen and be led
Only if we will be present, with open hearts and minds.

Waiting for what?
Reasons to take a critical stance for
Equity, justice, and freedom?
To be convinced that there are multiple ways of being and knowing?
To be convinced, finally, that it is true that "if they take you in the morning, they will be coming for us that night?"[2]
What are we waiting for?
Trayvon Benjamin Martin was murdered.
Breonna Taylor was murdered.
George Floyd was murdered.
What, again, are we waiting for?

Sandra Bland was murdered.
Walter Scott was murdered.
Alteria Woods was murdered.
Ahmaud Arbery was murdered.
India Kager was murdered.
And we watched and remembered others and
We cried and waited
For what?
By whom?
By when?

Engaged pedagogies mean that we are not waiting for . . . what?
Because engaged pedagogies summon us to the ground

To pause and listen to one another
To remain present and open and willing,
We are not waiting to name injustices, inequities, inequalities . . .
   again, *and*
To continue existing within oppressive spaces and places
Whether in schools and/or throughout society
That dehumanize and degrade
Demoralize and debase
Our human lives.

So, we must remain fully committed to:
Equity *and*
Justice *and*
Love *and*
Freedom *and*
Joy *and*
To our liberation and humanity *and*
To Black Lives Mattering.
No longer asking, "Waiting for what?"
Because we know the work is urgent for . . .

Chika, Ysende, and Jackson,
Sydney and Aliyah
Angela, Benjamin, and Aneesa
Todd, Brendan, and Jordan
Sarah, Tanya, and Kristopher
And for countless other children and young people
Who look to us to make things right
To make things just.
No longer asking, "Waiting for what?"
Because we know the work is urgent for . . .
Ms. Washington, Mr. Alston, and Ms. Streeter
Ms. donna Hicho
Ms. Davis, Mr. Merry, and Ms. Reed,
Ms. Rhonda Johnson
Ms. Mulvihill, Mr. Sapien, and Ms. Prince
Mr. Spears and Mrs. Penn
And for countless other educators and community organizers
Who are teaching and organizing
For positive change

For our lives to matter.

For families—our
Grandmothers, mothers, grandfathers, fathers, aunts
Children, nieces, nephews, uncles, other mothers, neighbors.
For organizers—of
Black Lives Matter movements
The #MeToo movement
LGBTQIA rights
Criminal justice reform efforts
Standing Rock and Indigenous rights movements
And all other movements committed to equity, justice, and anti-racism.

We do this work now!
We take up engaged pedagogies in practice
To fight back against the devaluing of public education
To change inequitable educational structures, policies, and cultures
Because we seek change that is inspiring
Because we commit to being in relation with others
Because we work with preservice teacher education students
And we need them to love, nurture, and honor children, youth, and families too.
Because we resist oppressive structures that will always maintain hostility and violence
Because we are from histories of oppression.

Because we have witnessed other testimonies of survival and have shared our own
As forms of engaged pedagogies
And because we have been and remain exhausted and hurt
We are no longer waiting . . . for what?
We are cultivating engaging spaces of learning within and beyond
Schools and classrooms
As we develop additional strategies for learning, living, loving, surviving, and thriving.
As we create opportunities for others to enter into this work, to lead this work
To build meaningful relationships with students and families.

As we invest in transformative teaching and learning.

As we rebuild public education into freedom portals.³
Waiting for what?
Engaged pedagogies and
Justice work with
Teachers *and*
Students *and*
Communities
Now.
Are you with us?
Let's go.
Together.

Notes

Chapter 1

1. We include our original found poetry throughout this book. For us, found poetry is a poetic collection of words, feelings, expressions, and memories gathered together from multiple sources—in our case, from our own words or snippets of what we (Valerie, Emily, Tamara, and Grace) have shared and discussed with one another. We create found poetry, which can also be referred to as word collages, as a way to deepen our connections with one another, with collaborators, with the experiences we have individually and collectively as we pursue justice in schools and communities, and with the impact of these engagements on how we enter and reenter the work. Found poetry is a form of hearing, remembering, and honoring the thoughts and emotions that are central to our work.

2. For inspiration, we turn to foundational examples from the Highlander Folk School (Glen, 1996), Citizenship Schools (Charron, 2009), and the Freedom Schools (Hale, 2016).

3. Throughout this book, we intentionally do not capitalize "white" as a way to decenter whiteness in humanizing ways. In doing so, we push back against standardized norms of academic writing and publishing that capitalize white and not any other descriptor, such as Black (see also Brunson et al., in press).

4. Many people use "folx" (and not the traditional "folks") as a way to signal inclusivity and criticality through and with language.

5. We are aware of many different attempts at school reform, restructuring, and improvement in this country. Such attempts (historical and contemporary) often render invisible the lives, literacies, desires, and dreams of the very people who should have access to better educational systems and networks. Our focus on engaged pedagogy serves as one way to situate equity, justice, liberation, and freedom in discussions about **rebuilding** schools: *what* schools are for and *for whom*. This connects to the importance of teaching and learning differently/within different systems.

6. For us, educators are students, teachers, administrators, families, community groups and organizations, and anyone else committed to justice teaching and learning in whatever spaces/places they find themselves.

Chapter 2

1. "Connected" is a pseudonym that we use to name the community organization where Ms. Hicho worked.
2. BLTL was funded by an initial $550,000 grant from Learn & Serve America/Corporation for National and Community Service. It was a partnership between the National Education Association (NEA) Foundation, a research university, and a teachers' union.

Chapter 5

1. According to estimates from the 2019 U.S. Census, Black people made up 13.4% of the U.S. population, Hispanic or Latinx made up 18.5%, and white people made up 76.3%. In both COVID number of cases and deaths, Black and Hispanic or Latinx people are over-represented proportionate to population size. The Centers for Disease Control and Prevention (CDC) reports that not all geographic areas are reporting data based on race and ethnicity, so these data are not generalizable to the entire U.S. population (September 17, 2020).
2. We are aware that some people have manipulated space-time dynamics (e.g., in boarding schools, with school bells, with seating students in desks in rows, etc.) and enacted forceful, dehumanizing schooling practices that restrict students' movements and explorations. We reject these practices in our call for refiguring schools and schooling into humanizing, equitable spaces and places.

Chapter 6

1. For current examples of students and teachers who actively fought against anti-Blackness and COVID-19, see the Heath High School junior who organized a Summer 2020 COVID-safe community forum to combat anti-Blackness. In addition, see the Black Lives Matter organizing effort at John Muir Elementary in Seattle that quickly spread across the entire district (Au & Hagopian, 2019).
2. The BLTL Symposium was a 2-day student-led conference. The event brought together teachers, students, families, community partners, researchers, and local legislators. Presenters publicly acknowledged their partners and shared larger lessons from their projects as forms of engaged teaching and learning as justice work.
3. See Chapter 3, in particular, for information about the Design Team, which was a leadership group formed at Liberty High School and under Ms. Washington's guidance.

Chapter 7

1. See bell hooks (1994), *Teaching to transgress: Education as the practice of freedom*. Routledge.

2. See James Baldwin's (November 1970) "An Open Letter to My Sister, Miss Angela Davis" published in *The New York Review*: https://www.nybooks.com/articles/1971/01/07/an-open-letter-to-my-sister-miss-angela-davis/.

3. We borrow Patrice Khan-Cullors' term, "freedom portal," which she discussed at the 2020 Annual Convention of the National Council of Teachers of English (see http//www.ncte.org).

References

Abod, J. (Director). (2002). *The edge of each other's battles: The vision of Audre Lorde* [Film]. Women Make Movies.
Abravanel, S. A. (2003). Building community through service-learning: The role of the Community partner [issue paper]. *Partnership/Community, 27*. https://digitalcommons.unomaha.edu/slcepartnerships/27
Adejumo, C. O. (2010). Promoting artistic and cultural development through service-learning and critical pedagogy in a low-income community art program. *Visual Arts Research, 36*(1), 23–34.
Alim, H. S., & Paris, D. (2018). What is culturally sustaining pedagogy and why does it matter? In D. Paris & H. S. Alim (Eds.), *Culturally sustaining pedagogies: Teaching and learning for justice in a changing world* (pp. 1–21). Teachers College Press.
Alund, N. N., Hineman, B., & Tamburin, A. (2020, June 4). Teenagers join pantheon of Nashville youth who harnessed peaceful protests to urge change. *Nashville Tennessean.* https://www.tennessean.com/story/news/local/2020/06/04/teens-lead-nashville-march-protest-george-floyd/3151774001/
Au, W. (2016). Social justice and resisting neoliberal education reform in the USA. *FORUM, 58*(3), 315–324.
Au, W., & Hagopian, J. (2019). How one elementary school sparked a city-wide movement to make Black students' lives matter. In L. Delpit (Ed.), *Teaching when the world is on fire* (pp. 95–107). The New Press.
Baker-Bell, A. (2020). *Linguistic Justice: Black language, literacy, identity, and pedagogy.* Routledge.
Baldridge, B. (2019). *Reclaiming community: Race and the uncertain future of youth work.* Stanford University Press.
Barad, K. (2013). Ma(r)king time: Material entanglements and re-memberings: Cutting together apart 1. In P. R. Carlile, D. Nicolini, A. Langley, & H. Tsoukas (Eds.), *How matter matters: Objects, artifacts, and materiality in organization studies.* Oxford Scholarship Online. https://oxford.universitypressscholarship.com/view/10.1093/acprof:oso/9780199671533.001.0001/acprof-9780199671533
Barrett, T., & Cohen, T. (2013, April 18). Senate rejects expanded gun background checks. *CNN.* https://www.cnn.com/2013/04/17/politics/senate-guns-vote/index.html

Bloome, D., & Egan-Roberston, A. (1993). The social construction of intertextuality in classroom reading and writing lessons. *Reading Research Quarterly*, 28(4), 305–333.

Boler, M. (1999). *Feeling power: Emotions and education*. Routledge.

Bowdon, M., Pigg, S., & Mansfield, L. P. (2014). Feminine and feminist ethics and service- learning site selection: The role of empathy. *Feminist Teacher*, 24(1–2), 57–82.

Brayboy, B., Gough, H., Leonard, B., Roehl, R., II, & Solyom, J. (2012). Reclaiming scholarship: Critical Indigenous research methodologies. In S. D. Lapan, M. T. Quartaroli, & F. J. Riemer (Eds.), *Qualitative research: An introduction to methods and designs* (pp. 423–450). Jossey-Bass.

Brooks, M. D. (2020). *Transforming literacy education for long-term English learners: Recognizing brilliance in the undervalued*. Routledge-NCTE.

Brown, L., & Strega, S. (2005). *Research as resistance: Critical, Indigenous and anti-oppressive approaches*. Canadian Scholars' Press.

Brunson, F., Graham, D., Burkhard, T., & Kinloch, V. (in press). Organizing for equity: Addressing institutional barriers and creating learning opportunities. In T. Akiva & K. H. Robinson (Eds.), *It takes an ecosystem: Understanding the people, places, and possibilities of learning and development across settings*. Information Age Publishing.

Buffenbarger, A. (2012, May 10). *Priority school educators are "Bringing Learning to Life."* National Education Association. http://priorityschools.org/engaged-families-and-communities/priority-school-educators-are-bringing-learning-to-life

Buras, K. L. (2020). *From Katrina to COVID-19: How disaster, federal neglect, and the market compound racial inequities*. National Education Policy Center. https://nepc.colorado.edu/sites/default/files/publications/PM%20Buras.pdf

Butin, D. W. (2003). Of what use is it? Multiple conceptualizations of service learning within education. *Teacher College Record*, 105(9), 1674–1692.

Butler, O. (1993). *Parable of the sower*. Grand Central Publishing.

Butler, T. (2017). "We need a song": Sustaining critical youth organizing literacies through world humanities. *Equity & Excellence in Education*, 50(1), 84–95.

Butler, T., Penn, J. I., & Merry, J. (2020). Pardon this disruption: Cultivating revolutionary civics through world humanities. In V. Kinloch, T. Burkhard, & C. Penn (Eds.), *Race, Justice and Activism in Literacy Instruction* (pp. 91–106). Teachers College Press.

Calderón, J. (Ed.). (2007). *Race, poverty, and social justice: Multidisciplinary perspectives through service learning*. Stylus.

Cammarota, J. (2011). From hopelessness to hope: Social justice pedagogy in urban education and youth development. *Urban Education*, 46(4), 828–844.

References

Caraballo, L., & Martinez, D. C. (2019). Leveraging language(s): Reframing rhetorics of fear with narratives of agency and hope. *Journal of Adolescent & Adult Literacy*, 63(1), 97–101.

Cargle, R. (2020, May 30). *Public address on revolution: Revolution now* [Video]. YouTube. https://www.youtube.com/watch?v=leBPMyQ60HM

Carruthers, C. (2018). *Unapologetic: A Black, queer, and feminist mandate for radical movements*. Beacon Press.

Centers for Disease Control and Prevention. (2020, September 17). *Demographic trends of COVID-19 cases and deaths in the US reported to CDC*. https://covid.cdc.gov/covid-data-tracker/

Charron, K. M. (2009). *Freedom's teacher: The life of Septima Clark*. University of North Carolina Press.

Clark, S. P., & Brown, C. S. (1986). *Ready from within: Septima Clark and the civil rights movement*. Wild Trees Press.

Collins, P. H. (1990). *Black feminist thought: Knowledge, consciousness, and the politics of empowerment*. Routledge.

Combahee River Collective Statement. (1971). In B. Guy-Sheftall (Ed.), *Words of fire: An anthology of African-American feminist thought* (pp. 232–240). The New Press.

Daniel, J., Welner, K. G., & Valladares, M. R. (2016). *Time for improvement: Research-based expectations for implementation of the community schools initiative in New York City*. National Education Policy Center. http://nepc.colorado.edu/files/publications/PM%20Daniel%20Community%20Schools_0.pdf

Davies, K. (2019). 'Sticky' proximities: Sibling relationships and education. *Sociological Review*, 67(1), 210–225.

Denzin, N. K., & Lincoln, Y. S. (2005). Introduction: The discipline and practice of qualitative research. In N. K. Denzin & Y. S. Lincoln (Eds.), *The SAGE handbook of qualitative research* (pp. 1–32). SAGE.

Dimitriadis, G. (2001). Coming clean at the hyphen: Ethics and dialogue at a local community center. *Qualitative Inquiry*, 7(5), 578-597.

Dyson, M. E. (2006). *Come hell or high water: Hurricane Katrina and the color of disaster*. Basic Civitas.

Eagle Shield, A., Paris, D., Paris, R., & San Pedro, T. (2020). *Education in movement spaces: Standing rock to Chicago freedom square*. Routledge.

Ella T. v. State of California, No. BC685730 (Cal. Super Ct., 2017). https://media2.mofo.com/documents/171205-ellla-t-v-california-complaint.pdf

Ellsworth, E. (2004). *Places of learning: Media, architecture, and pedagogy*. Routledge.

Elrick, M. L., & Robinson, E. (2020, June 6). Macomb County's Hall Road protest started with iMessages between 3 teen girls. *Detroit Free Press*. https://www.freep.com/story/news/local/michigan/macomb/2020/06/06/black-lives-matter-macomb-march/3163465001/

Everytown. (n.d.). *Background checks on all gun sales.* https://everytown.org/solutions/background-checks/

Everytown. (2019, February 11). *Gunfire on school grounds in the United States.* https://maps.everytownresearch.org/gunfire-in-school/#17079

Fine, M. (2018). *Just research in contentious times: Widening the methodological imagination.* Teachers College Press.

Fothergill, A., & Peek, L. (2012). Permanent temporariness: Displaced children in Louisiana. In L. Weber and L. Peek (Eds.), *Displaced: Life in the Katrina diaspora* (pp. 119–143). University of Texas Press.

Francesca, C. [@chiara.acu]. (2020, December 18). *A love letter for the solstice and the new year* [Post]. Instagram. https://www.instagram.com/p/CI98YcYFjgp/

Freire, P. (2000). *Pedagogy of the oppressed.* Continuum Publishing Company.

Gary B. v. Snyder, No. 16-CV-13292, (E.D. Mich. 2016). https://www.detroitaccesstoliteracy.org/wp-content/uploads/2016/09/2016-09-13-Complaint.pdf

Garza, A. (2020). *The purpose of power: How we come together when we fall apart.* One World.

George, T. (Director). (2004). *Hotel Rwanda* [Film]. Lions Gate Entertainment Films.

Glen, J. M. (1996). *Highlander: No Ordinary School* (2nd ed.). University of Tennessee Press.

Greene, M. (1995). *Releasing the imagination: Essays on education, the arts, and social change.* Jossey-Bass.

Hale, J. N. (2016). *The Freedom Schools: Student activists in the Mississippi civil rights movement.* Columbia University Press.

Hari, J. (2018). *Lost connections: Uncovering the real causes of depression—and the unexpected solutions.* Bloomsbury.

Hart, S. (2006). Breaking literacy boundaries through critical service-learning: Education for the silenced and marginalized. *Mentoring & Tutoring, 14*(1), 17–32.

hooks, b. (1981). *Yearning: Race, gender, and cultural politics.* South End Press.

hooks, b. (1994). *Teaching to transgress: Education as the practice of freedom.* Routledge.

hooks, b. (2010). *Teaching critical thinking: Practical wisdom.* Routledge.

hooks, b. (2018). *All about love: New visions.* William Morrow Paperbacks.

Horton, M., Kohl, J., & Kohl, H. (1998). *The long haul: An autobiography.* Teachers College Press.

Hutton, B. (2020). "We have to talk about liberating minds": Angela Davis' quotes on freedom. AnOther Magazine. https://www.anothermag.com/design-living/12607/angela-davis-quotes-on-freedom-juneteenth-black-lives-matter-movement

Ishimaru, A. M., Bang, M., Valladares, M. R., Nolan, C. M., Tavares, H., Rajendran, A., & Chang, K. (2019). *Recasting families and communities as co-designers of education in tumultuous times*. National Education Policy Center and Family Leadership Design Collaborative. https://nepc.colorado.edu/publication/family-leadership

Jones, A., & Jenkins, K. (2008). Rethinking collaboration: Working the indigene-colonizer hyphen. In N. K. Denzin, Y. S. Lincoln, & L. T. Tuhiwai Smith (Eds.), *Handbook of critical and Indigenous methodologies* (pp. 471–486). SAGE Publications.

Jordan, J. (2002). *Some of us did not die: New and selected essays of June Jordan*. Basic/Civitas Books.

Kaye, C. B. (2010). *The complete guide to service learning: Proven, practical ways to engage students in civic responsibility, academic curriculum, & social action*. Free Spirit Publishing.

Keating, A. (2013). *Transformation now! Toward a post-oppositional politics of change*. University of Illinois Press.

Kinloch, V. (2009). Suspicious spatial distinctions: Literacy research with students across school and community contexts. *Written Communication, 26*(2), 154–182.

Kinloch, V. (2010). *Harlem on our minds*. Teachers College Press.

Kinloch, V. (2016). *Diversity, equity, and inclusion: A position statement for colleges of education*. Ohio State University. http://static.ehe.osu.edu/downloads/diversity/EHE-DICE-Position-Statement.pdf

Kinloch, V. (2017). "You ain't makin' me write": Culturally sustaining pedagogies and Black youths' performances of resistance. In D. Paris & H. S. Alim (Eds.), *Culturally sustaining pedagogies: Teaching and learning for justice in a changing world* (pp. 25–41). Teachers College Press.

Kinloch, V. (2018). Necessary disruptions: Examining justice, engagement, and humanizing approaches to teaching and teacher education [Working paper]. *TeachingWorks Working Papers*, 1–23. https://www.teachingworks.org/images/files/TeachingWorks_Kinloch.pdf

Kinloch, V., Nemeth, E., & Patterson, A. (2015). Reframing service-learning as learning and participation with urban youth. *Theory Into Practice, 54*(1), 39–46.

Kinloch, V., Penn, C., & Burkhard, T. (2020). Black lives matter: Storying, identities, and counternarratives. *Journal of Literacy Research, 52*(4), 382–405.

Kinloch, V., & Smagorinsky, P. (Eds.). (2014). *Service-learning in literacy education: Possibilities of teaching and learning*. Information Age Publishing.

Kirp, D. L. (2016). How to fix the country's failing schools. And how not to. *The New York Times*. http://www.nytimes.com/2016/01/10/opinion/sunday/how-to-fix-the-countrys-failing-schools-and-how-not-to.html

Ladson-Billings, G. (2006). From the achievement gap to the education debt: Understanding achievement in U.S. schools. *Educational Researcher, 35*(7), 3–12.

Ladson-Billings, G., & Tate, W. F. (1995). Toward a critical race theory of education. *Teachers College Record, 97*(1), 47–68.

Langstraat, L., & Bowdon, M. (2011). Service-learning and critical emotion studies: On the perils of empathy and the politics of compassion. *Michigan Journal of Community Service Learning*, 5–14.

Laparra, N. (Host). (2020, June 9). Teens4Equality—How six teens organized the largest Black Lives Matter protest in Nashville [Audio podcast episode]. In *Let's Give a Damn*. https://www.nicklaparra.com/episodes/teens4equality

Lave, J., & Wenger, E. (1991). *Situated learning: Legitimate peripheral participation*. Cambridge University Press.

Lemke, J. L. (2000). Across the scales of time: Artifacts, activities, and meanings in ecosocial systems. *Mind, Culture, and Activity, 7*(4), 273–290.

Lesko, N. (2012). *Act your age! A cultural construction of adolescence* (2nd ed.). Routledge.

Li Sui, G. [@gweezilla]. (2018, February 23). *Gun violence haiku* [Photograph]. Instagram. Retrieved from https://www.instagram.com/p/Bfg3qS8hbZ5/?utm_source=ig_embed

Lorde, A. (1984). *Sister outsider: Essays and speeches*. Ten Speed Press.

Love, B. (2019). *We want to do more than survive: Abolitionist teaching and the pursuit of educational freedom*. Beacon Press.

Lyiscott, J. (2014, February). *3 ways to speak English* [Video]. TED Conferences. https://www.ted.com/talks/jamila_lyiscott_3_ways_to_speak_english?language=en

Marino, D. (1998). *Wild garden: Art, education, and the culture of resistance*. Between the Lines.

Maybach, C. W. (1996). Investigating urban community needs: Service learning from a social justice perspective. *Education and Urban Society, 28*(2), 224–236.

Mirra, N. (2018). *Educating for empathy: Literacy learning and civic engagement*. Teachers College Press.

Mitchell, T. (2007). Critical service-learning as social justice education: A case study of the citizen scholars program. *Equity & Excellence in Education, 40*(2), 101–112.

Morris, M. (2018). *Pushout: The criminalization of Black girls in schools*. The New Press.

Mosley, T., & McMahon, S. (2021, February 8). *Fighting for the right to literacy in Detroit* [Radio broadcast]. WBUR. https://www.wbur.org/hereandnow/2021/02/08/right-to-literacy-michigan

Muhammad, G. (2020). *Cultivating genius: An equity framework for culturally and historically responsive literacy*. Scholastic.

Mulligan, M., & Nadarajah, Y. (2008). Working on the sustainability of local communities with a "community-engaged" research methodology. *Local Environment, 13*(2), 81–94.

References

Muñoz, J. (2009). *Cruising utopia. The then and there of queer futurity*. NYU Press.

National Alliance for Public Charter Schools. (2015). Michigan: No caps. National Alliance for Public Charter Schools. https://www.publiccharters.org/node/1431

Nemeth, E. A. (2017). *Engaged pedagogies: communities working toward collective agency* [Unpublished paper]. National Council of Teachers of English Annual Convention.

Nemeth, E. A., & Winterbottom, C. (2016). Communities of practice: Youth and social justice service-learning. In A. S. Tinkler, B. E. Tinkler, V. M. Jagla, & J. R. Strait (Eds), *Service learning to advance justice in a time of radical inequality*, pp. 299–319. Information Age Publishing.

Nemeth, E. A., Butler, T., Kinloch, V., Washington, T., & Reed, P. (2014). Transformative service-learning in urban schools and communities: Learning from challenges. In V. Kinloch & P. Smagorinsky (Eds.), *Service-learning in literacy education: Possibilities of teaching and learning* (pp. 3–26). Information Age Publishing.

New England Resource Center for Higher Education. (2018). *Carnegie Foundation Community Engagement Classification*. https://nerche.org/carnegie-engagement-classification/

Nyachae, T. (2019). Social justice literacy workshop for critical dialogue. *Journal of Adolescent and Adult Literacy*, 63(1), 106–110.

Ohito, E., & Nyachae, T. (2019). Poetically poking at language and power: Using Black feminist poetry to conduct rigorous feminist critical discourse analysis. *Qualitative Inquiry*, 25(9–10), 839–850.

Orfield, G. (2014). Tenth annual *Brown* lecture in education research: A new civil rights agenda for American education. *Educational Researcher*, 43(6), 273–292.

Paris, D. (2012). Culturally sustaining pedagogy: A needed change in stance, terminology, and practice. *Educational Researcher*, 41(3), 93–97.

Patel, L. (2016). Pedagogies of resistance and survivance: Learning as Marronage. *Equity & Excellence in Education*, 49(4), 397–401.

Patterson, A., Kinloch, V., & Nemeth, E. (2017). The stories they tell: Giving, receiving, and engaged scholarship with/in urban communities. *eJournal of Public Affairs*, 6(2).

Player, G. D., & Ybarra, M. G. (2021). Reimagining literacy and language education for Girls of Color. *Urban Education*, 1–10.

Price-Dennis, D. (2019). "What happens here can change the world": Preparing literacy teachers in the digital age. In V. Kinloch, T. Burkhard, & C. Penn (Eds.), *Research on race, justice, and activism in literacy teacher education* (pp. 23–34). Teachers College Press.

Reed, P., & Butler, T. (2014). Flipping the script: When service-learning recipients become service-learning givers. *Theory Into Practice*, 54(1), 55–62.

Reich, J. A., & Wadsworth, M. (2008). Out of the floodwaters, but not yet on dry ground: Experiences of displacement and adjustment in adolescents and their parents following Hurricane Katrina. *Children, Youth and Environments, 18*, 354–370.

Renkl, M. (2020, June 15). These kids are done waiting for change. *The New York Times.* https://www.nytimes.com/2020/06/15/opinion/nashville-teens-protests.html

Rosenberger, C. (2000). Beyond empathy: Developing critical consciousness through service-learning. In C. R. O'Grady (Ed.), *Integrating service-learning and multicultural education in colleges and universities* (pp. 23–44). Lawrence Erlbaum Associates.

San Pedro, T., & Kinloch, V. (2017). Toward projects in humanization: Co-creating and sustaining dialogic relationships [Centennial Issue]. *American Educational Research Journal, 54*(1S), 373S–394S.

Satrapi, M. (2003). *The Complete Persepolis.* Pantheon.

Shange, S. (2019). Black girl ordinary: Flesh, carcerality and the refusal of ethnography. *Transforming Anthropology, 27*(1), 3–21.

Sharpe, C. (2016). *In the wake: On being and blackness.* Duke University Press.

Smith, B. (1989). A press of our own kitchen table: Women of Color Press. *Frontiers: A Journal of Women Studies, 10*(3), 11–13.

Swaminathan R. (2005). "Whose school is it anyway?" Student voices in an urban classroom. In D. W. Butin (Ed.), *Service-learning in higher education: Critical issues and directions* (pp. 25–43). Palgrave Macmillan.

Taylor, K. Y. (2020). Reality has endorsed Bernie Sanders. *The New Yorker.* https://www.newyorker.com/news/our-columnists/reality-has-endorsed-bernie-sanders

Tennessean. (2020, June 4). *Local teens are leading a Black Lives Matter protest in Nashville* [Video]. YouTube. https://www.youtube.com/watch?v=ufL1pyJiPjM

Torrez, J. E., Gonzales, L., Del Hierro, V., Ramos, S., & Cuevas, E. (2019). Comunidad de cuentistas: Making space for Indigenous and Latinx storytellers. *English Journal, 108*(3), 44–50.

Tretheway, N. (2008). THE GULF: A meditation on the Mississippi coast after Katrina. *The Virginia Quarterly Review, 84*(3), 4–27.

Tuck, E., & Yang, K. W. (2013). New studies in youth resistance: Introduction to Part III. In K. W. Yang & E. Tuck (Eds.), *Youth resistance research and theories of change* (pp. 177–180). Routledge.

U.S. Census Bureau. (2020). Quick facts. https://www.census.gov/quickfacts/fact/table/US/PST045219

Williams v. Reeves, No. 3:17-cv-404 WHB-LRA (S.D. Miss., 2017). https://www.splcenter.org/sites/default/files/documents/indigo_williams_et_al_v_phil_bryant_et_al_complaint.pdf

Wisely, J. (2020a, April 23). Appeals court finds constitutional right to literacy for schoolchildren in Detroit case. *Detroit Free Press.* https://www.freep.com/story/news/education/2020/04/23/literacy-right-constitution-detroit-schools/3011945001/

References

Wisely, J. (2020b, May 20). Despite settlement, Detroit literacy lawsuit heads back to court. *Detroit Free Press*. https://www.freep.com/story/news/education/2020/05/19/federal-appeals-court-overturns-detroit-literacy-lawsuit-ruling/5225188002/

Wolf, M. (2018). *Reader come home: The reading brain in a digital world*. HarperCollins.

Zernike, K. (2016, June 28). A sea of charter schools in Detroit leaves students adrift. *New York Times*. https://www.nytimes.com/2016/06/29/us/for-detroits-children-more-school-choice-but-not-better-schools.html

Index

Abod, J., 137
Abravanel, S. A., 29
Adams, John, 25
Adejumo, C. O., 41
Alim, H. S., 3
Alund, N. N., 75
Au, W., 60, 154

Baker, Ella, 123
Baker-Bell, A., 8
Baldridge, B., 78
Bang, M., 57
Barad, K., 96
Barrett, T., 134
Basic minimum education right, 6–7
"Being Radical" (poem), 94
Belyue, Ariana, 75
A Better Us (BLTL projects), 36, 47
Beyond the Black Berry Patch project, 36–37
Black Feminist Thought (Collins), 29
Black Lives Matter (BLM) movement, 75–76
Blacks, 2
 and performances of resistance, 4
Bland, Sandra, 33
Blankets for Babies (BLTL projects), 43–44
BLM (painting), 77
Bloome, D., 67
Boler, M., 50, 64, 66, 67, 68, 69, 70
Book Buddies (BLTL projects), 36, 43
Bowdon, M., 63, 64, 65, 68
Boyd, Rekia, 35
Brayboy, B., 15

Bridging the Gap: Linking the Generations Through Service to All (BLTL projects), 44
Bringing Learning to Life (BLTL) initiative, 23–47, 124
 critical service-learning and engagement projects, 42–47
 events occurred during and after course, 33, 35
 invitations, 124–126
 Justice High School and, 83–84
 in larger context, 32–35
 overview of, 28–32
 on positionality, 37–39
 projects, overview of, 35–37
 session at Connected, 25–28
 texts in, variety of, 41–42
 World Humanities classroom and, 84–87
Brooks, M. D., 8
Brown, C. S., 7
Brown, Chris, 88
Brown, L., 15
Brown v. Board of Education, 6
Brunson, F., 153
Buffenbarger, A., 12
Bullying, 38
Buras, K. L., 98
Burkhard, T., 16, 153
Butin, D. W., 63
Butler, O., 65
Butler, T., 17, 38, 60, 65, 78, 84, 90

Calderón, J., 41
Cammarota, J., 41
Campus-Wide Recycling (BLTL projects), 47

Cans for the Canopy: Kids, Cans, Conservation project, 37
Caraballo, Limarys, 8
Carey, Miriam, 35
Cargle, R., 70
Carruthers, C., 88
Carthan, Eddie James, 101
Catalytic empathy, 66–67
Chang, K., 57
"Change, Changes, Changing" (poem), 74
Change, learning and, 14
Charron, K. M., 153
Cheadle, Don, 62
Citizenship School movement, 61
Civil rights' educators, 100–101
Clarity, upheaval and moments of, 96–100
Clark, S. P., 7, 100
Cohen, T., 134
Collaboration, 11–12, 23, 37, 123
  collective desire to, 12–14
Collaborative school change, 15
Collins, Nya, 75
Collins, P. H., 29, 30
Combahee River Collective (CRC), 87
Community Art Service-Learning Lessons (BLTL projects), 44–45
Community-engaged initiative, 26, 42–47
Community Garden (painting), 71
Community of practice, 12–13
  formation of, 50
  role of empathy in, 50–51
The Complete Guide to Service Learning: Proven, Practical Ways to Engage Students in Civic Responsibility, Academic Curriculum, & Social Action (Kaye), 29
The Complete Persepolis (Satrapi), 84
Connected (nonprofit community development organization), 23–25
  BLTL session at, 25–28
COVID-19 global pandemic, 97–100
Critical service-learning projects, 26, 38, 42–47
  empathy in, 63–64
  examples of, 36–37

Critical youth organizing literacies (CYOL), 78–79
  imagination, 80–83
  time travel, 79–80
Cuevas, E., 16
Cyberbullying, 87, 88–91

Daniel, J., 9, 15
Davies, K., 130, 131
Davis, Angela, 123
Del Hierro, V., 16
Denzin, N. K., 16
Design Team/Team, 53–60
DeVos, Betsy, 9–10
Dimitriadis, G., 51
Disability Awareness Campaign, 40–41, 58, 60
Disengagement, 131–133
Dombrowski, James A., 61
Dreaming (painting), 2
Duggan, Mike, 7
Dyson, M. E., 96

Educational policy reform, 4–10
Educational survival complex, 10, 81
Egan-Roberston, A., 67
Elementary school projects, 42–44
Ellsworth, E., 58, 66, 70
Elrick, M. L., 75
Emily (painting), 142
Empathetic leadership, 60–65
Empathetic readings in literature, 64–65
Empathy, 63–65
  catalytic, 66–67
  continuum of, 69–70
  role in community, 50–51
Engaged learning, 91–93
Engaged pedagogy, 2–4
  features of, 51
  paradoxes of, 117–120
  physicalness of, 116
  in practice, 23–47
English language arts (ELA), 28
Essential Workers (painting), 98
Everytown, 134, 136

Fine, M., 53, 70
Fleischman, Paul, 52

Index

Fothergill, A., 96
Francesca, Chiara, 136
Fraternal proximities, 128–131
Freedom, 11–12, 38, 136
Freedom School movement, 101
Freire, P., 58, 124
Fuller, Jade, 75
Futures, envisioning, 109–110
Fye, Michelle, 36

Garfield High School, 6
Gary B. v. Snyder, 6
Garza, A., 125
Glen, J. M., 153
Glover, Danny, 96–97
Gonzales, L., 16
Good Seeds Community Garden (BLTL projects), 46
Gough, H., 15
Grace (painting), 143
Graham, D., 153
Gray, Freddie, 33
Gray, Kimani, 35
Great Lakes Education Project, 9
Green, Kennedy, 75
Greene, M., 39, 41, 92
Grimes, Erica, 36

Hagopian, J., 154
Hale, J. N., 101, 153
Hallway (painting), 59
Hari, J., 117
Hart, S., 41
Hicho, donna, 23, 26–27, 39
Highlander Folk School, 61–63
High school projects, 46–47
Hineman, B., 75
hooks, b., 1, 2, 3, 4, 39, 96
Horton, M., 61, 66
Horton, Myles, 61, 100–101
Hotel Rwanda (film), 62, 67
Hurricane Katrina, 96–97
Hutton, B., 11
Hyphenating literacies, 50, 53–60

I Am You (painting), 92
I Can Empower Change (BLTL projects), 44
Imagination, 80–83

Indigenous people, 2
Integrating Nature (BLTL projects), 45
Ishimaru, A. M., 57

Jenkins, K., 53, 67, 70
Johnson, Rhonda, 39
Jones, A., 53, 67, 70
Jordan, J., 41
Junk values, 117
Justice High School, 83–84

Kaye, C. B., 29
Keating, A., 123, 126
Kinloch, V., 3, 8, 12, 14, 16, 38, 53, 60, 67, 70, 91, 153
Kirp, D. L., 15
Kitchen Table (painting), 24
Kohl, H., 61, 66
Kohl, J., 61, 66

Ladson-Billings, G., 9, 41
Landscapes, ruptured, 91–93
Langstraat, L., 63, 65, 68
Latinos y CSIA: Construyendo Puentes de Salud (Latinos and CSIA: Building Health Bridges) project, 36
Latinx, 2, 36
Lau v. Nichols, 6
Lave, J., 12, 53
Layering of time, 107–109
Leaders/leadership, 57
  empathetic, 60–65
  for social change, 61
Learning, 14
  and change, 14
  collaborative, 83–84
  engaged, 91–93
  organizing, 117
  purposes of, 13–14
Learningscapes, 102–104
  expanded, 115–116
  organic, 126–128
Lemke, J. L., 107
Leonard, B., 15
Lesko, N., 102
Liberty High School, 61–62, 70–72
Lincoln, Y. S., 16
Li Sui, G., 136
Literacies, hyphenating, 50, 53–60

Living Healthy (BLTL projects), 42–43
Lorde, A., 8, 88, 137, 141, 145
Love, B., 5, 10, 61, 81
Lyiscott , J., 8

Mama Protester (painting), 5
Mansfield, L. P., 64
March for justice, 75–76
Marino, D., 126
Marti, Trayvon Benjamin, 35
Martinez, Danny C., 8
Masterful weavers, educators as, 120–121
Master of divinity (MDiv), 105
Maybach, C. W., 29
McMahon, S., 7
Measures of Academic Progress (MAP) test, 6
Merry, J., 36, 84, 90
Metaphors, 56
Middle school projects, 44–46
Mirra, N., 50, 66, 69, 70
Mitchell, Arelya, 101
Mitchell, T., 41
Monae, Janelle, 89–90
Morris, M., 61
Mosley, T., 7
"Moving, Even in Stillness" (poem), 140
Muhammad, G., 8
Mulligan, M., 37
Mulvihill, Antonia, 37
Muñoz, J., 101
Mutual participation, 2

Nadarajah, Y., 37
National Education Association (NEA), 28, 130
Neighborhood pride, 88–91
Nemeth, E., 13, 60, 67
Nemeth, E. A., 38, 60, 66
Newark City School system, 15
Nieves-Ferguson, Brenda, 36
Nolan, C. M., 57
Nyachae, T., 18, 81, 141, 145

Obama, Barack H., 33, 90
Ohito, E., 18, 141, 145

Olamina, Lauren, 65
"On Not Waiting" (poem), 22
Openness, 67–70
Orfield, G., 9, 10

Parable of the Sower (Butler), 66
Paris, D., 3, 8, 10
Paris, Rae, 8
Participation
  mutual, 2
  purposes of, 14
Partnerships, 36
  purposes of, 14
Patel, L., 8, 9, 14
Patterson, A., 13, 60, 67
Pedro, Timothy San, 8
Peek, L., 96
Penn, C., 16
Penn, J. I., 84, 90
Physicalness, 116
Pigg, S., 64
Player, Grace D., 2, 8, 24, 34, 55, 59, 71, 77, 82, 92, 98, 112, 118, 138, 142–143
Positionality, 37–39
Power drill, 133–136
Price-Dennis, Detra, 8
Pride, neighborhood, 88–91
Private interest groups, 8–9
Protect Black Femmes (painting), 118
Public school reforms, 6

Race/racism, 9–10
Radical interconnectedness, 123
Rajendran, A., 57
Ramos, S., 16
Reading Mentors (BLTL projects), 45–46
Reading Mentors project, 36
"Really Not Waiting" (poem), 122
Recycled Urban Art (BLTL projects), 45
Reed, Pam, 25–26, 27–28, 37–39, 38
Reforms, educational policy, 4–10
Reich, J. A., 96
Relational networks, 116
Relationships
  repairing, 60
  with students, 31

Index

Renkl, Margaret, 75, 76
Resistance, performances of, 3–4
Resourcing engagement, 113
Restoration, 70–72
Retention, engagement as, 131–133
Robinson, Bernice, 100
Robinson, E., 75
Roehl, R., II, 15
Roots & Seeds (painting), 138
Rosenberger, C., 63–64, 70
Ruptured landscapes, 91–93
Rusesabagina, Paul, 62

San Pedro, T., 8, 14, 16
Santana, Angel, 75
Satrapi, Marjane, 84
School change, collaborative, 15
Science, Technology, Engineering, and Mathematics (STEM) academy, 23–24
Scott, Walter, 35
Seedfolks (Fleischman), 52
Shange, S., 80, 81
Sharpe, C., 90
Shield, Alayna Eagle, 8
Smagorinsky, P., 38
Smith, B., 88
Smith, Emma Rose, 75
Smith, Mikayla, 75
Social ills, 68–69
Social justice, 85–86, 90–91, 123
Solyom, J., 15
Space, reconfiguration, 111–115
Spaces for engagement, 37
Spanish FLEX (language experience mentoring project) (BLTL projects), 46
"Stand Up/Speak Out" project, 38
Stevenson, George, 25
Still I Rise (BLTL projects), 43
Stoop (painting), 13
Streeter, Shawna, 26
Strega, S., 15
Swaminathan, R., 41

Tamara (painting), 143
Tamburin, A., 75
Tate, W. F., 41

Tavares, H., 57
Taylor, Breonna, 76
Taylor, K. Y., 96
Teachers & Students (painting), 40
Teens for Equality, 75
Tensions, 117
Thomas, Zee, 75, 78
Time
  layering of, 107–109
  reconfiguration of, 104–110
Time travel, 79–80
Torrez, J. E., 16
Transformations, of schools, 10–14
Trayvon (painting), 34
Tretheway, Natasha, 97
Tuck, E., 78

Union City School system, 15

Valerie (painting), 142
Valladares, M. R., 9, 15, 57
Visions for Justice (painting), 112
Vucaj, Mary, 75

Wadsworth, M., 96
"Waiting for . . . ?" (poem), 48, 141–151
Washington, T., 38
Water, Water, Everywhere (BLTL projects), 46–47
We Deserve (painting), 82
We Do It for the Community (painting), 55
Wellspring, of energy/creativity/excitement, 119–120
Welner, K. G., 9, 15
West, Don, 61
Winterbottom, C., 60
Wisely, J., 7
Wolf, M., 64, 65, 67
World Humanities classroom, 90, 92
  BLTL and, 84–87

Yang, K. W., 78
Ybarra, Mónica González, 8

Zernike, K., 9
Zero tolerance discipline policies, 1, 2

About the Authors

Valerie Kinloch, the NCTE president from November 2021–November 2022, was born and raised in Charleston, South Carolina, and she completed her K–12 education in public schools there. She earned her undergraduate degree from Johnson C. Smith University, and her graduate degrees from Wayne State University. A literacy scholar, educator, and higher education leader, Kinloch's scholarship examines the literacies and engagements of youth and adults in school and community spaces. Author of publications on race, place, literacy, and equity, she has written books, articles, and chapters on poet June Jordan, on critical perspectives related to language and learning, and on community engagement.

Emily Nemeth is an associate professor in the Department of Education at Denison University, where she teaches courses on literacies, gender and sexualities, critical approaches to teaching and learning, and qualitative research methodologies. Her research explores the design of, and meaning-making possibilities within, engaged pedagogies in schools and community spaces. As an engaged teacher-scholar, Nemeth currently works with The Freedom School in Licking County, the Community Alliance for Racial Justice, and the Children's Defense Fund Freedom Schools of Licking County in the state of Ohio.

Tamara T. Butler is an educator from Johns Island, South Carolina, who enjoys learning from plants, podcasts, and creatives. Currently, she serves as the executive director of the Avery Research Center for African American History & Culture and associate dean of Libraries at the College of Charleston. Her research on Black Girl literacies and justice-oriented education has been published in a variety of outlets and has shaped her ongoing project (BlackGirlLand) and connections to life stories and creative works.

Grace D. Player's work is rooted in her experiences as an Asian American Woman of Color, a daughter to an immigrant woman, and a sister to many. She is a literacy scholar, educator, and artist who has a longstanding commitment to collaborating with Communities of Color. Player's research and practice take on a Feminist of Color lens and are aimed at collaborating with Girls and Women of Color to better understand how they mobilize their raced, gendered, and cultural knowledges and ways of knowing to forge sisterhoods that resist injustice and transform worlds.